Confessions of a

Silk Road User

Life on the Road

Ronald Stark

Confessions of a Silk Road User
Life on the Road

ISBN: 978-0-578-12388-2

This book has been written, detailing a minor portion of one man's experience with using the hidden online marketplace. This book contains strong language and suggestive themes. This book was written for entertainment purposes only and should not be used otherwise.

TABLE OF CONTENTS

A FEW QUOTES I FIND MEANINGFUL ENOUGH TO PUT AT THE FRONT OF MY BOOK!

Read these quotes over a blunt of weed or a tab of LSD to really absorb it man. Not really. Don't do drugs, drugs are bad. They make you think. Whether it be paranoid thinking, or coming to terms with life and reality. I'm just kidding. Choosing to do drugs is your decision to make. I simply ask you do your research and make smart and safe decisions. But my lawyers insist you don't do anything illegal because you read any part of this book. So after reading this book in part or in whole then you may not participate in any type of illegal activity. If you however find my book helpful or entertaining please send me a donation in bitcoins! Here is an address which you may use: 19D4qJK2tmfgNN8quiPX6pq6tDSig2J6ww

1. The Federal Reserve System relies on the force of government to maintain it's monopoly power on the issuance of money. This is how all central banks maintain their control. Without the state's involvement, people would be free to use whatever currency they like. Historically this was gold. If the founders of the fed tried to do what they did w/o the Federal Reserve Act legislation, and later the Brenton Woods agreement, they would have failed miserably. No one would have bought into their system.

In fact, this is the beauty of libertarianism. The people are free to choose what system they want. No need for one size fits all government solutions. If you want to use a debt based inflationary monetary system, go right ahead, doesn't affect me so long as you don't try to force me to use it as well. – Dread Pirate Roberts

2. None of us would remember as we were not born, but the railroad companies in the 19th century used to pay their workers in currency that was only good at company-owned stores. These were the days before the dollar was standardized as a currency, and what would happen is that the RR companies controlled their workforce - the workers could not buy food & clothing anywhere else unless the RR owned it. As I recall from reading American History books (in grade school or some other distant young age) this was some of the reasoning for standardizing or strengthening the dollar - so that it could be used across society and to promote free enterprise as opposed to issuing certificates again usable only in businesses wholly run by the rail companies. Mostly these

workers got food, clothes, whiskey & whores only, neverthe-less, they couldn't use these certificates anywhere else. Like working at a Wal-mart and being paid with Wal-mart gift cards good for purchases only at a Wal-mart. – unknown

3.   *Wise criminals are safe criminals.- unknown*

4.   *A fool who, after plain warning, persists in dosing himself with dangerous drugs should be free to do so, for his death is a benefit to the race in general. - H.L. Mencken*

5.   *In 1980, there were 315,974 [inmates in American state and federal prisons]; in 1981, there were 353,674, an increase of 10 percent; and in 1982, there were 396,072, another 11 percent. Suppose this same growth curve continues, so that we add 12 percent the next year, 13 percent the following, and so on. In the year 2012, 415,389,484 Americans will be in state and federal prisons. Now that is a frightening prospect, particularly granted that the total U.S. population projected for that year is only about 315,000,000. Apparently we're going to have to find an extra hundred million people just to fill our prisons; and that doesn't even address the question of who will guard us all. - Population Growth as Blessing or Blight, E. Calvin Beisner, attempting to point out a statistical absurdity, but also demonstrating just how quickly the war on drugs has expanded our prison population.*

6.   *Although drugs are immoral and must be kept from the young, thousands of schools pressure parents to give the*

drug Ritalin to any lively child who may, sensibly, show signs of boredom in his classroom. Ritalin renders the child docile if not comatose. Side effects? "Stunted growth, facial tics, agitation and aggression, insomnia, appetite loss, headaches, stomach pains and seizures." Marijuana would be far less harmful. - Gore Vidal, THE WAR AT HOME, November 1998

7. Suppose that the US really is trying to get rid of drugs in Colombia. Does Colombia then have the right to fumigate tobacco farms in Kentucky? They are producing a lethal substance far more dangerous than cocaine. More Colombians die from tobacco-related illnesses than Americans die from cocaine. Of course, Colombia has no right to do that. - Noam Chomsky, Noam Chomsky on the Drug-Terror Link, By Philip Smith, DRCNet, February 14, 2002

8. It is possible to stop most drug addiction in the United States within a very short time. Simply make all drugs available and sell them at cost. Label each drug with a precise description of what effect - good or bad - the drug will have on the taker. This will require heroic honesty. Don't say that marijuana is addictive or dangerous when it is neither, as millions of people know -- unlike "speed," which kills most unpleasantly, or heroin, which can be addictive and difficult to kick. Along with exhortation and warning, it might be good for our citizens to recall (or learn for the first time) that the United States was the creation of men who believed that each person has the right to do what he wants with his own life

as long as he does not interfere with his neighbors' pursuit of happiness (that his neighbor's idea of happiness is persecuting others does confuse matters a bit). . - Gore Vidal, 1970

9. *There are no violent gangs fighting over aspirin territories. There are no violent gangs fighting over whisky territories or computer territories or anything else that's legal. There are only criminal gangs fighting over territories covering drugs, gambling, prostitution, and other victimless crimes. Making a non-violent activity a crime creates a black market, which attracts criminals and gangs, which turns what was once a relatively harmless activity affecting a small group of people into a widespread epidemic of drug use and gang warfare. - Harry Brown, Libertarian Party*

10. *I didn't inhale. – Bill Clinton*

11. *To fight and conquer in all your battles is not supreme excellence; supreme excellence consists in breaking the enemy's resistance without fighting. - Art of War, Sun-Tzu, Chapter 2, Paragraph 2*

12. *Strict gun laws are about as effective as strict drug laws...It pains me to say this, but the NRA seems to be right: The cities and states that have the toughest gun laws have the most murder and mayhem. - Mike Royko, Chicago Tribune*

13. *I know not too many people are going to like the fact that I published this book. I don't care, its my right to do so. But when you*

think about it I did a huge favor in expanding the community to this revolutionary new way of expressing freedom known as The Silk Road. – The author of this book. March 2013

That concludes the interesting and possibly thought provoking quotes I have decided to include in my book. You may proceed, to read. Live life and have a good time indeed. Like a ganja farmer planting some weed, the Road to riches, will start from a seed.

DISCLAIMER

This book has been written and published for entertainment purposes only. This book is in no way shape or form meant to be used as a guide to ANYTHING! This book goes into detail about how an underground marketplace for illicit substances operates. If you plan on using any part of this book to commit a crime or violation of law then you should not have bought this book in the first place. If you are unsure about what activity constitutes a crime or violation of law then I ask that you please consult a lawyer or your local, state, and federal statutes regarding the activity in question.

Upon purchasing this book you agree to not hold me, the author of this book responsible for anything. I do not know you so there is no reason you should hold me accountable for your future actions after having read this book in its entirety or in part. This book was written for entertainment purposes only and any information contained within its pages should not be taken seriously and/or applied to real life scenarios.

The information in this book may not be used to commit a crime. You have been warned. My aim in writing this book and compiling the information between its pages was merely to tell a fictional story regarding use of the online marketplace known as The Silk Road by a fictional character. My story is fictional and any similarity or likeness to an actual person, place, or thing is purely coincidental. If you do not believe me then simply go online and read the forums and you will find out how ridiculously easy it is to write this story simply by learning a few tips.

Drugs are bad!!!

Upon purchasing this book you agree that you have not purchased this book for anyone who you might suspect, even slightly suspect of using this book to commit a crime or violation of law.

INTRODUCTION

Before I begin let me say that a great investment opportunity exist in Bitcoin and the medical marijuana industry. You can be a part of these revolutions by simply investing in them. I have tripled my original investment already in Medical Marijuana Inc. (MJNA) and increased my original investment in Bitcoins by more than several hundred times. Get with it before it's too late!

----BEGIN PGP MESSAGE-----

Version: GnuPG v2.0.19 (MingW32)

hQEMA2Svq0ISVIenAQfdxyGfjTJBd+kfVIIy60
0Ms2/7PmND+O3PcNrdqLFEVQunjxnEi/ZH
2tSRpYUINWpMA9uDeFL86gHAa1pWkM+7
7vppYaeiNIH8vHilXE8+NhjC6MnRYSZ94iCy

3 X 1 7 3 W T 9 5 G k v Z Q q F Y q k 5 y o 9 i c
0vP5xbp4o8ilWRcT7l3OHlqAbkJXoz3K6plvTGX6t
CjcwtKfZ7o1v4p6yh3xCkHopjqpt/v86RGMHdNPqi
XghfOdFekMnCrF8T/CI1h0fYgwntBUHIuj
QHGRwdnv54N+6PXpYn1HYJfHw7i1I
War+uuEg08j93isyOhxR8Z6gw11r8C5
Oh1o32mJ11HcZh0P09LACwG+3AWW4ZJ1pF1tN
Ojd1GEwvhF3NJXrWsP6O8dwrZJuEVcXIoK4V5ro0
j+1iEk2m6+1BE1XO0wjZGyiFpLPx7AZRMo5NQa
XxbYRzpo59VcvkTs1l4wqV6ym4ZEn4lFXPheozxtz
J6cKt6qEl6nI7n1keS0U+/C8C6QpPdmMLDh7P9Ivy
0IvrdxzKmw48gvIDoJaHBWJ6ygzY9Y1bl4nkEbMxg
53Ye2HdiAZY0WBbPY15VC6ZupPSgBw2psgezvIaYJK
ApdwchezOxo=E8ed

-----END PGP MESSAGE-----

I apologize in advance for any downtime to the website in relation to any potential swarm of new users.

I would like to welcome you all to my book. My goal in writing this book is to expand the community and its ideals by getting the word out about how to access the Silk Road Marketplace. If you don't know what I mean by community I mean the on-line drug marketplace, aka Silk Road.This is a community of people who have came together to slap the face of discrimination by dealing a blow to the war on drugs. This great invention shouldn't be limited to a few people who tempt fate and risk jail time by ordering from this site. This website should be made legal and we should bring about an end to the war on drugs. We should not be scared to break the law because we want to experience drugs. Alcohol and tobacco are legal yet they have proven to be more deadly than most, if not every other drug. So why can't we have safe access to our drug of choice? Ordering from this unique, revolutionary website ensures I won't get robbed or possibly hurt trying to pick up some weed or pills like I risk when I meet someone in person.

Its ridiculous that they cant seem to stop the flow of illegal drugs yet have not attempted to regulate them with taxes and limitations on amounts that can be purchased. Its crazy weed isn't legal in all 50 states yet either. I have a feeling that will happen within the next 10 years as more and more states are putting votes on the ballots. If I had to pick the first few drugs to be completely legalized and taxed like alcohol and tobacco I would vote for weed, LSD, shrooms, and MDMA. What would you pick?

I have been an avid Silk Road user ever since August of 2012. Since I first read about it on the internet and until today I still cannot believe a technological masterpiece like this exists. This is definitely a huge blow to the war on drugs. I congratulate the creators for making this website. You should too. Visit the site and you will see what I mean. It is allowing people to step out of the shadows and up to the mailbox to buy and sell drugs.

The Road has changed my life in both positive and negative ways. It's not as bad as some people think. I have definitely had my bills paid on time. I have supplied hundreds if not thousands of people in my county and surrounding counties with good times and cheap party substances.(Cheaper in my county as I sell to resellers and my resellers sell to resellers, the price of course goes up.) The thrill of riding around in a rolling drug store half the day and filling my wallet back up is truly priceless. You should try it sometime.

Another thing that is truly priceless is opening the mail box and finding packages of blotters, two types of ecstasy and a quarter pound of weed! That day felt like fucking Christmas because I didn't expect them to arrive on the same day but on three separate days. I never imagined I would end up like this. I still wish I could predict the future. Not just having déjà vu. I hate that shit when it happens. I mean like really predict the future. I can somewhat predict the future because of one simple fact: I'm not selling anymore. Don't call or text me. I sold my methods of using The Road to my top resellers and they are on their own now.

If you didn't get the invite then you are doing something wrong or I just don't like you. But here's your chance if you read this book. I felt it was time to leave this shit alone because I had heard from a confidential source that a 14 year old kid had gotten hurt tripping his brains out and ended up in the hospital. He didn't get it from me but rather a reseller of one of my resellers. I hope you go down so hard for that. No one is selling to you right now because of that. You were told the rules ahead of time and you fucked it up by selling to kids. I have no sympathy for you when it comes to your bills or food. You got greedy and sold to somebody who wasn't smart or old enough to make a logical decision regarding drugs.

I'm a drug dealer but I have a heart. I wouldn't want somebody selling shit to my kid unless it was weed which is why in my ring everything else besides weed is off limits to young people. I know, I know, if I had a heart I would never have sold drugs. Well FYI I don't consider weed, LSD, MDMA drugs as long as they are used in a controlled environment for therapeutic purposes. Yes they can be therapeutic. I didn't always think like this. I have sold cocaine and Nbome as well. That was because of greed and I don't condone the use of these two substances any more.

Throughout this book you may stop and think, this dude goes off track sometimes and rants about stuff. I'm sorry. Get over it and read the whole thing. I feel like it is my book and I have the right to express some of my feelings no matter what the topic.

I am comfortable where I am in life right now and no longer feel a need to obtain drugs in my mail box. I can't risk anymore harm to myself or family and am currently living a drug free life(with exception to cannabis!) This has been a crazy ride from beginning to end. I thank the creators of the Silk Road Marketplace for allowing me to experience a great form of freedom that has been oppressed for many years. The freedom to experiment with whatever substances I want to. To all the law enforcement officials I have evaded with my tactics of doing business I say this, and I quote" I'm laughin straight to the bank with this, ha ha ha ha, ha, ha ha ha ha ha." – 50 cent

Shout out to my loyal customers and friends!: To those of you who have had too good of a time because of the Nbome,LSD, and shrooms(the ones who take shits in front of mailboxes at four in the morning or throw pieces of used lumber through the windows of passing cop cars☺) I say this: LOL! Don't text me shit like that, just tell me in person. To those of you who cant seem to bust a nut because of the bk-MDMA and the MDMA I say this: Give her a break!To those of you who have abandoned your alternate high grade weed dealer because of my lower prices I say this: Don't tell the other dealers who you are getting it from now, are you trying to make Johnny Blazed kill a fool?! And stop smoking and driving!!!To those of you who have had your bills paid on time because of my system of doing business, I say this: No need to thank me, just follow the rules we agreed upon and nobody goes to jail! To those of you who bought this book I say this: Thank you very much for your contribution to the Johnny Blazed Foundation. This donation is NOT tax deductible. I wish you luck on your journey down the Silk Road, thanks again. To my loving family members who have put up with my bullshit, I say this: Thanks for staying by my side, no matter what kind of trouble I got in, you guys always provided a shoulder to lean on, I love you!

I'm sorry if you become bored while reading my book. I have also supplied you guys with some drug safety information and some great tips about receiving drugs at home safely. To those of you who have decided you'd rather not buy drugs through the mail but start sending drugs through the mail, for profit or not, there are some great tips on how to succeed in that as well. As this book ages you may find it necessary to consult more up to date information on the topic of drugs in the mail, as law enforcement and drug dealers play a constant cat and mouse game for superiority. It is up to you to make smart choices. Stay safe.

CHAPTER 1

A LAZY OVERVIEW OF THE ROAD AND ITS USE

In this chapter I have written up a basic method of using the site. Please use the most up to date methods to use the site by visiting the sites forums. To use the forums you first have to follow my instructions on accessing the website. Once you have created an anonymous account you may use the sites forums by scrolling to the bottom of the page and clicking on the Community Forums link.

According to Wikipedia the Silk Road or Silk Route is a modern term referring to a historical network of interlinking trade routes across the Afro-Eurasian landmass that connected East, South, and Western Asia with the Mediterranean and European world, as well as parts of North and East Africa. Today however the Silk Road has taken on a new meaning. The Silk Road I speak of is the online marketplace where illicit substances can be bought and delivered just about any-where in the world. Most drug users aren't aware of this. I can tell because bit coins aren't as expensive as they could be! Bit coins? I'll get to that later.

The website and people behind it are revolutionaries in many ways. The greatest thing in my opinion however that they have accomplished, with exception to the hopefully lifetime supply of MDMA I currently own, would be that people will always choose to find a release from everyday life through drugs, that being said the Silk Road has made it safe for the seller and buyer in regards to the violence sometimes associated with face-to-face drug deals. You can buy a few grams (or a pound!) of weed from your recliner and have it delivered to your mailbox or front door within a few days! How awesome is that? Seriously, answer me! Okay, okay, you're not a pothead. Maybe crack-cocaine floats your boat. Maybe you your used to getting is. Maybe it's been years since you went to a Grateful Dead show and you no longer have a contact for LSD. Perhaps your diet and exercise regimen are not enough to keep you packing on pounds of muscle at the gym, oral and injectable steroids are just a few clicks away! Go ahead and make those balls disappear! Don't forget your grandpas' birthday is coming up and he has a thing about going to the doctor for his erectile dysfunction. Viagra anyone? These are just a small percentage of the drugs that can be purchased safely from the comfort of your own home. Did I forget to mention that there are private areas of the website where bulk drugs can be bought if you meet certain criteria, the World is yours you little, entrepreneurial, drug dealer you!

It is somewhat difficult at first to access the website and purchase bit coins (the digital currency that allows for strong anonymity if bought correctly) First you have to download TOR. TOR stands for The Onion Router. No it doesn't make you cry (unless you get caught using it in China!) It offers layers of protection, get it? According to Wikipedia it is a system intended to enable online anonymity. Tor client software directs internet traffic through a worldwide volunteer network of servers to conceal a user's location or usage from anyone conducting network surveillance or traffic analysis. Using Tor makes it more difficult to trace internet activity, including "visits to web sites, online posts, instant messages and other communication forms", back to the user and is intended to protect users' personal privacy, freedom, and ability to conduct confidential business by keeping their internet activities from being monitored.

TOR is fairly safe to use to buy happiness (your drugs!) as long as no one knows what you're doing, you don't access websites like PayPal, your personal banks website, or something like Facebook where your personal information is available then your experience buying drugs online should be secure. Just remember that the Silk Road is heavily monitored so be careful about what sites you connect to after your visit on the website. It is possible for someone to figure out what you are doing if you visit a site where your personal information is stored.

Bitcoins, bitcoins, and more bitcoins! Dread Pirate Roberts probably feels like Donkey Kong or Super Mario with all the coins he's getting! I know I do (actually I'm speculating because of the release of this book!)" Evil laugh!(fuck E-Trade!) Evil laugh!" Bitcoins are the currency of the online black market and as previously stated are great investments. They do have legal purposes too which is why they shouldn't be out lawed. Bit coins can be directly purchased with your personal information or without. You might want to do it without your personal information that way when they become taxed you don't have to answer the question the IRS is going to ask you: "Well Johnny Do-good, where did all those bit coins you purchased on Mt.Gox go?" "I smoked them in my bong of course!" Fail! Don't let that happen to you. Get your ass to the nearest MoneyPak distributor and max that sucker out, GPS the next location and max another card out! There are several ways to purchase them, cash deposits at banks, MoneyPak, websites that require identification. Just check out the Silk Road forums for the latest and up to date methods. I'm retired because I have made quite a bit of money in a short time, the legal ramifications of the business I was conducted could have landed me in jail for life, and I was able to make some legal investments to supplement my income. I have also had the opportunity to purchase a house with some land and am now a certifiable pothead, I grow in my greenhouse.

The only way to have drugs successfully land in your mailbox without you having to sign to get raped (controlled delivery) is to choose a reliable vendor. Check out their feedback and look at the forums and asking longtime users for advice is a good idea. If their packaging methods are not up to par they will be intercepted and you will definitely hear about it from the Postal Service. Either through a letter stating your package was returned to sender because of inadequate postage or the package was too suspicious and opened for inspection. Either way your address will be monitored, especially when some grandma in Nice town gets a package filled with ketamine because her address was used as the return address and your dumbass used a fake name or abandoned address to receive the package at. Receiving packages at home is ballsy but can be done safely.

Make sure your house is not the neighborhood drug superstore and is already under surveillance, make sure your house is clean from other illegal items, and use a name associated with that address. The mailman will notice something wrong if The Buttsniffers residence gets a package addressed to the Buttlickers. Ya see what I'm getting at. EVERYTHING has to appear as normal as possible for your experience to be successful. Just don't get crazy like me and order $19000 worth of merchandise in 36 packages within my first 2 months, just from the website. I bullshit you not. It is extremely easy to make some fast money if you know a bunch of people. Hell if you knew one person that knows a bunch of people then just wholesale to them. I thought you had to keep them coming. I have so much bullshit from eBay it's not even funny anymore. I have bought almost every shirt under the funny t-shirt category it's ridiculous. You don't have to do this but I felt like I got in too deep and felt like if I stopped having a few packages arrive every week they would put the zoom on me because deliveries would be very inconsistent. Especially since some of my PO boxes were setup to receive business names. Vendors on the road who have a moderate level of intelligence will never require you to sign for a package(international orders are probably the only exception) If you are expecting a package that day and your mailman comes to the door asking you to sign for it then your goose is cooked. Don't open that door even if it's a sweet mail lady with perky tits. If they ask you to sign for it then you are basically admitting you knew you were getting something that day. Most mail delivery personnel are in a hurry and won't waste time ringing the bell more than once. They aren't UPS or FedEx and most packages do not require a signature.(especially ones containing drugs fool!) If you've had a postal employee come to your door on a day you were expecting a drug delivery I would advise you to not open the door at all, clean your house, and count that one as a loss. I would also be cautious about ordering more packages to that address because you are potentially being watched.

So you've figured out how to install TOR on your computer and you have located the hidden URL to access Silk Road, now it's time to see what all the fuss is about. Let's Enter The

Matrix! Where we are free to do as we like without being persecuted. You can't fly or bend backwards to dodge bullets but you can order a lifetime supply of prison!(Only if you are caught!)I'm still good. Thousands of other people are still walking among the rest of us as well. When you first visit there will be a login screen and you will need to setup a new account. Just follow the onscreen instructions and choose a username and password you have NEVER used before or anything that is related to you or can be traced back to you! Duhhhhh! Unless you want to see vendors from all over the world choose your home country (domestic). Click submit and wait for the page to load! TOR is somewhat slow and impossible to connect to at times as you will figure out but is well worth it, just ask my bank account!

OMG! It's finally here! I did it! Do you see all the cat-egories and subcategories of drugs! Holy shit! I've got to tell Timmy to throw in with me on a quarter pound! SSSSSSSTTTTTTTTTOOOOOOOOOOOPPPPPPP right there mister! Don't tell a soul that you are using the site! "Can you keep a secret?""Yeah why?""Me too!" Hush yo mouth fool! Do the Helen Keller! Zips yo lips! If anybody is curious about your newly found, very reasonably priced drug dealer and why they can't meet him or buy from him just tell them," cuz he told me not to let anybody know who he is dude!" Simple as that. Eventually The Road will be as popular as MySpace, yet still somewhat forgotten and not talked about!"Slap!" That was the sound of Mark Zuckerberg high-fiving me! Basically you get an idea of what you want to buy, add it to your cart,(OMG it's like a real website)if you haven't already deposited into your account figure about how much you will need and deposit a little extra to compensate for fluctuations in the value of bitcoins, which can vary widely over the course of a day! Once your funds are in your account and are ready to purchase there is one more step to ensure safety on your end. "WTF!" I'm sorry but this step is not necessary to complete a transaction it did however let me sleep good at night on the days leading up to expected packages of MDMA and cocaine! In the address field there is a space for your address. You will want to encrypt your address using PGP and copy/paste it into this field. Simply find out how to download a free PGP program from the Silk Road forums, visit the vendors' page of your selected item and download their public key into your PGP program. To encrypt a message PGP uses two parts. A public key and a private key. Never hand out your private key! It's called private for a reason! Simply type your message and then select encrypt and choose your vendors public key. Voila! Copy and Paste this scrambled mess of random numbers, letters, and characters into the address field and click submit. Now wait. Your package should be at its destination in a matter of days! From your orders page you will see all pending transactions. There is a button called finalize, never under any circumstances press this button UNTIL your order arrives and you confirm its contents! If you finalize without having your order in hand then you risk getting scammed. There is no way for the sites escrow system to protect you if you FE. (Finalize early) Read the forums fool!

The day has finally come! Its 11:15 a.m. and you see the mailman making his rounds! You piss your pants, now go inside and change and stay there until he has placed it into your mailbox and drives outta sight. The less people that see you grabbing the mail the better. Just make sure you get it before your mom or dad does and ask you what's in it or opens it for you. I don't condone anyone living at home or kids receiving packages. If this applies to you then think about the complications that could arise if something went wrong. You don't want the cops busting you and your mom telling them," yeah he was expecting a skateboard magazine" Then they WILL know for sure you were expecting a package and your plausible deniability will plummet! Plausiwhat ? Read the forums fool! Read the forums before you even place your first order. You will learn a lot. You will also learn how to encrypt your computer so it will be better protected if the cops think to start searching it. This chapter was a lazy overview of how to successfully use the Silk Road Marketplace. Please consult the Silk Road forums for up to date information on its use. I will probably also write a chapter later in this book with a more detailed instruction on successful use. Stay tuned and I hope you enjoy the rest of my book(even the ones that want me dead because of this book) as I account for some of my experiences from the Road and how it has changed my life in both positive and negative ways. No matter the outcome I am glad for having discovered this wonderful website, even though I have had some close calls in regards to selling IRL because of it. If any of you vendors happen to find out my SR username and for whatever reason remember one of the addresses I used then I urge you to reconsider searching for me. You will be met with disappointment in the guise of a …… Ima stop right there because I am a convicted felon and do not have any weapons.

Here below you will find a few pages of my imagination at play. I'm very good at reading people, kind of like a psychic. So here is my interpretation of how the USPS operates in regards to drug packages. And before you ask here is my answer: " no I did not hack into the FBI's computers or infiltrate the USPS in any way to obtain this information."

Screening of packages does not take place every day of the week by Postal inspectors. This is only done if they have information that a large shipment of drugs or other contraband is coming through. The only exception to this would be at your country's customs where drug dogs, x-rays, and random screenings are used every day. You shouldn't be too concerned about your package getting intercepted. If you are receiving envelopes then they should be made out to a business name if they are to be frequent deliveries. These usually never get x-rayed. Larger, suspicious looking packages are what you need to be worried about. If a dog alerts on a package, that's going to be x-rayed as well.

Dogs are used for random screenings and once the package is alerted on by a dog and x-rayed to confirm possible contraband, the inspectors get a warrant and go through a lengthy process of discreetly opening it (documenting it with video or still photos all the way) in such a way that will allow them to repackage it for a controlled delivery, if they decide to make one. Seized packages tended to have a lot of drugs in them- there aren't many small packages. Seized packages almost always consist of something like this: some type masking agent is used to hide the smell, like big jars of peanut butter, a big teddy bear stuffed with drugs, and a lot of steroid packages that simply broke in transit and leaked all over the box. Any leaking or other staining on the outside of the package is a huge flag.

Don't worry, most weed vendors triple vacuum seal your nuggets and it is somewhat impossible to detect unless the package looks fucked up on the outside. However it is only a matter of time before the smell escapes even from that. Many vacuum sealed bags of weed are intercepted because of shipping delays or the vacuum for whatever reason opened up. The less time your package spends in the postal system, the better off you are.

The only time where a regular looking letter or envelope would possibly be inspected would be either because it was sent as media mail (cheap ass postage) or because the sender or recipient is already suspected of some other crime, usually but not limited to: child pornography, work from home scams, advance fee scams where one guy is getting hundreds of letters stuffed with cash sent to his house every day. Most normal, law abiding Americans use the U.S. Postal Service nearly every day. Whether to send bills to clients, advertise for new customers, or exchange letters with friends, citizens rely on the Postal Service to help them conduct their professional and personal business. Some people on the other hand use it to conduct business in the drug trade. Either by sending cash or drugs. In Omaha, Nebraska, authorities have taken steps to cut off the drug trade conducted by mail. In 1988. inspectors from the U.S. Postal Inspection Service proposed a partnership with the Omaha, Nebraska, Police Department's Narcotics Unit to interdict drugs transported into the city by mail. Prior intelligence gathering revealed that dealers smuggled large amounts of cocaine into Omaha simply by wrapping up the drugs and mailing them at the post office. Smugglers often used express delivery methods because the demands of quick delivery lowered the chances of detection by postal inspectors.

The joint operation has yielded positive results. In one case, inspectors intercepted a suspicious package mailed from Los Angeles, California, to an Omaha address. Based on the subsequent investigation, inspectors obtained a search warrant for the package, which contained 6 ounces of powdered cocaine. The drugs led the joint team to a big arrest when an undercover postal inspector made a controlled delivery of the package to the mailing address in Omaha, and police officers immediately executed a search warrant on the location. Inside, officers apprehended a hard core gang member who had relocated from southern California and established gun- and drug-running operations in the city. The success of this operation and others like it stemmed from two factors: Use of a package profile to identify suspicious parcels and close cooperation between the U.S. Postal Inspection Service and the Omaha Police Narcotics Unit during the investigatory process.

Based on my experience, there are several methods by which a postal inspector uses to identify contraband in the mail. To identify pieces of mail that might contain controlled substances, postal inspectors rely on a package profile based on a readily discernible, predetermined set of criteria. Past court decisions make clear that the regular application of a consistent set of criteria is not intrusive. Using the profile helps establish reasonable suspicion, which is required by the Postal Service to detain mail for examination.

The profile sets criteria for both the package's condition and its label. Taken individually, few of the criteria would indicate that the package contains contraband; however, a combination of these factors indicates a suspicious package worthy of a second look. Some of this stuff is a no-brainer. In order for a package to get through to its destination it needs to look and feel normal.

First, in terms of the package itself, inspectors look for parcels that have been heavily taped along the seams, have been prepared poorly for mailing, have an uneven weight distribution, or apparently have been reused. However, inspectors do not identify questionable pieces of mail only by sight; suspicious packages frequently emit odors of marijuana or of a masking agent, such as perfume, coffee, or fabric-softener sheets.

Second, package labels often provide clues. Inspectors look for labels that have been handwritten; contain misspelled names, streets, or cities; originate from a drug-source State; and have been sent from one person to another, not from a business to an individual. Further identifiers include a return address ZIP code that does not match the accepting post office ZIP code or a fictitious return address. Finally, the names of the sender and/or the receiver frequently have a common ring to them, such as John Smith, and have no connection to either address. Basically you don't want any misspelled names on your bundle of weed because the mailman will know better and the package might not get through next time. Vendors on the Road usually copy and paste your address and print it out. That label is then applied to the package. Person to person is ok every now and then. If you make it a habit then you might be setting yourself up for failure. I used several business names when I received mail at Post offices. This ensured me weekly deliveries of product because I mean seriously, what individual gets packages every week without being involved in some type of legal business?

Postal inspectors receive copies of all labels from packages signed for by the recipient. If a particular address receives multiple deliveries from a drug-source State, for example, inspectors will check with postal carriers at both the sending and receiving addresses to verify names and addresses. If the return address is fictitious or if the listed names do not have a connection to either address, inspectors will be alert to intercept future packages. It is generally in your best interest to purchase from a vendor who doesn't use fake return addresses. As long as you do your part and don't use a fake or odd-sounding receiving name, or attempt to have the package sent to an abandoned building then there is no reason for your deliveries to appear suspicious. Remember not to let your mailman or anybody else see you picking the package off the porch or out the mailbox. "Hey he got a similar one last week, I seen him grab it myself!" "why the hell is he not opening the door for us then?" The Postal Inspection Service bears responsibility for detecting suspicious packages. This type of investigation requires patience, because inspectors routinely examine hundreds of mailing labels on packages sent through the mail. Through these examinations, inspectors attempt to recognize packages matching the profile characteristics. When they locate a suspicious package, the investigation begins.

Upon discovery of a suspicious package, postal inspectors notify the local Police Narcotics Unit. The unit's supervisor assigns a drug dog handler to meet with the inspector and present the package to the dog. Presentation strategies vary. Sometimes the handler hides the package to see if the dog can sniff out its location. At other times, the handler presents the suspicious package to the dog, along with other similar parcels. If the dog alerts then you are fucked. Smart vendors are up to par with defeating drug dogs. This can be accomplished by foil packaging in addition to the normal vacuum sealing procedures. Sterilization of the outer container is also necessary because the dog can pick up on the little bit of cocaine that fell out of your nose when you sneezed while dropping the package off at the post office. The dog handler carefully records the details of the presentation for future use as search warrant documentation. The dog's positive reaction to the package indicates the presence of drugs, which in many cases establishes probable cause to prepare a search warrant to inspect the parcel's contents.

Suspicious package investigations typically require two search warrants: One to open and search the package and one to search the mailing address after delivery of the parcel. Postal inspectors and police investigators work closely to ensure that all documentation for the warrants is complete and accurate, important factors in obtaining evidence and prosecuting the case. It is somewhat hard for some people to have absolutely clean homes while they either purchase drugs through the mail or use them on a daily basis. If you are receiving packages at your home then you need to do this: Upon receiving a package place contents into a new container and dispose of all shipping materials including envelopes, boxes, papers, postage, and any type of container that the drugs were housed in during shipping. That way if you are raided during a controlled delivery then you stand a decent chance in defeating the charge of receiving drugs in the mail because you will not have similar packaging laying around that can be linked to the new package. You might still be fucked if they search your computer and find that you visited the site because you are too lazy to encrypt your computer. I use a laptop and I know where to hide it. It only comes out when I ordered new product.

Because the U.S. mail falls under Federal jurisdiction, a Federal warrant must be obtained for any suspicious package. The police drug dog handler helps the inspector prepare the affidavit because they must provide the magistrate with a history of the dog's reliability and past achievements. If Lucky can sniff the dimebag you hid behind your gascap then he can sniff out that dimebag hidden in that flat rate box. Dogs can smell regular vacuum sealed nuggets and other drugs. It is vital to package drugs with foil that has to be heat sealed, kinda like the material they use to make chip bags.

Having obtained the warrant, postal inspectors open the package. This important step must not be dealt with carelessly. The package might need to be resealed for a controlled delivery, so inspectors must exercise caution. To preserve fingerprints on any item or contraband, the person opening the package wears rubber gloves. Inspectors also photograph the opening of the parcel in a series of steps for use as future evidence. Usually vendors on the road,(the more intelligent ones) make the packaging so that if opened it would be very difficult to not tear accidentally and reseal without having the recipient know. Of course the postal inspector could simply print out a new shipping label if he had to. You probably wouldn't be none the wiser.

In the formative stages of Omaha's drug interception program, postal inspectors and police investigators met with prosecutors to determine a strategy for handling cases brought by the joint team. They concurred that when a package containing drugs was identified, investigators would remove most of the drugs, leaving just a small amount to be resealed in the package and delivered later. Prosecutors agreed that they could argue successfully in court that the defendant found in possession of the resealed package actually had "constructive possession" of the original amount of contraband. However, to preserve the elements of the State or Federal drugs violation, it would be best if at least some of the drugs originally seized were delivered in the package.

After removing most of the illegal substance, inspectors frequently replace it with an imitation so as not to alert suspects when they open the package. For example, a recent investigation in Omaha located a large amount of crack cocaine formed into the shape of cookies. Investigators left several of the original crack cookies in the package but substituted sugar cookies for the rest.

On a practical note, this procedure safeguards against the loss of the evidence in the unlikely event that the subject eludes police officers after the package is delivered but before the search warrant of the residence can be executed.Officers quickly discovered that suspects often attempt to leave the location with the evidence immediately following the controlled delivery of the package but prior to the entry team's arrival. The pit bulls in your back yard would come in handy right now as they probably wouldn't allow a police officer to wait for you to come running out the back door with the evidence.

Once the package has been searched and resealed, the Police Narcotics Unit supervisor prepares a search warrant for the mailing address. This does not have to be a Federal warrant, but the Federal search warrant used to open the package is referenced in the warrant petition and a copy is attached.

A police investigator and the postal inspector collaborate to prepare the second search warrant. The affidavit describes exactly how the investigation began--with discovery of the suspicious package--and follows with the details of presenting the parcel to the drug dog, obtaining the Federal search warrant, opening the package, and locating the drugs. The affidavit also notes that officers removed a specific amount of the drug from the package, left a small amount, and refilled the package with an imitation substance.

This type of search warrant is anticipatory in nature. That is, the affidavit clearly must show that law enforcement officers currently possess the drugs to be seized and that they intend to serve the search warrant after the controlled delivery of the package. If probable cause exists, items such as packaging materials, scales, long distance telephone bills, money, drug records, and additional drugs should be listed on the warrant to be seized. Any historical or intelligence information about the address of the anticipated delivery or the persons known to frequent the address also should be documented in the affidavit. This is why a clean house is necessary. You will probably need a burner phone that is not linked to your name or address to if you plan on reselling.

The next step involves delivering the package to the intended address under carefully controlled conditions. The Narcotics Unit supervisor handles three aspects of this operation. The supervisor arranges the controlled delivery, establishes a secure perimeter around the address to prevent the subject from leaving with the package, and supervises the execution of the search warrant.

First, the supervisor conducts an extensive reconnaissance of the address, especially noting all possible exits. Because at least several minutes will elapse between the controlled delivery and the execution of the search warrant to allow the recipient time to open the package, all exits of the address must be placed under surveillance to prevent anyone from leaving with the package. A great place to hide shit is in the insulation of an attic. I usually go as far away from the attic entrance as possible and store valuables. It gets kind of hot in the summer time so your drugs might go bad depending on what they are. Yes drugs can go bad. Especially weed and LSD if left in the heat.

Second, the supervisor briefs all officers involved in executing the search warrant, dividing officers between the perimeter and entry teams. The perimeter team, which keeps all exits of the target address under surveillance, must be positioned to stop and arrest anyone who might leave with the package after it has been delivered. The entry team, which typically comprises Omaha police officers, postal inspectors, and occasionally, FBI agents, serves the warrant, makes appropriate arrests, and conducts the subsequent search of the premises.

An undercover postal inspector normally delivers the package after the perimeter team takes its position. In most situations, the Narcotics Unit supervisor then gives the recipient enough time to open the package, because an opened package undermines the commonly used defense that the suspect did not know what it contained.

In addition, experience shows that the original recipient often will turn over the parcel to a second person who arrives within minutes of the delivery. For this reason, the supervisor might choose to wait a considerable length of time before sending in the entry team. At the appropriate time, the entry team executes the search warrant for the package on the target location. During the search, officers remain alert for additional drugs, drug records, money, long distance telephone bills, scales, baggies, and other labels of packages previously mailed to the address, as listed on the warrant.

Upon completion of the search, the supervisor quickly analyzes the situation to determine whether to interrogate the person who signed for the package on the scene. If such questioning could prove fruitful, the suspect is advised of his Miranda rights. On occasion, by immediately interrogating the recipient, investigators have convinced suspects to make tape-recorded telephone contact with a second suspect who, in turn, arrived at the scene only to be arrested.

Investigators question the arrested parties thoroughly to determine their knowledge of the parcel's contents and their connections with a network of people involved in smuggling the package into the city. Many postal profiling cases in Omaha have resulted in Federal prosecution of individuals in other States, such as California, for participating in drug smuggling operations. The only problem with Silk Road deliveries is that there is no one you can snitch on if you get caught. It's not like you are going to tell them you got it online. The best thing you can do in regards to snitching would be to work with them and take down some other local dealers. If you get caught with a bunch of LSD or MDMA you can pretty much kiss life as you know it goodbye. If you have a great knowledge of where some cocaine, crack, or other hard drugs can be bought in town then this is your best chance to have your charges lessened or dropped completely. If they don't ask you to help out in exchange for something then have your lawyer ask them if they would be willing to obtain your help. Your lawyer is still your best friend if you become a confidential informant.

The success of the package profiling program in Omaha proves that law enforcement can transcend jurisdictional boundaries to combat crimes that often go undetected. Highlights of the program include two separate seizures of 3-pound quantities of crack cocaine valued at approximately $250,000 each that had been mailed to Omaha from sources in Los Angeles. Tyrone would have a heart attack if he seen a huge rock like that!

Not all seizures have run smoothly. In one case, inspectors intercepted a package containing 5 ounces of methamphetamine. Following standard procedure, officers removed all but 5 grams of the substance, which they sealed in a tube taped to the inside of the package. A female at the target address signed for the package during the controlled delivery, but when officers executed the search warrant, no drugs could be found. Knowing that they had delivered the methamphetamine, officers conducted an extensive and thorough search of the premises but to no avail. Finally, several hours later, the woman vomited the tube intact. She had swallowed it when she saw the law enforcement officers approach the residence.

Despite the occasional mishap, the package profiling system has produced many seizures that have netted both crack and powdered cocaine, marijuana, LSD, methamphetamine, heroin, steroids, and hallucinogenic mushrooms. Prosecutors have obtained numerous felony convictions in both Federal and State courts. Profiling postal packages represents a challenging and exciting aspect of drug enforcement. In the future, law enforcement agencies might expand the use of this technique to detect packages transported by private carriers and parcel services.

The expertise gained by working with postal inspectors to detect controlled substances sent by mail could be applied to private carriers in an attempt to choke off other conduits for transporting controlled substances. By employing every method available, U.S. Postal Inspectors can work with local law enforcement agencies to keep the Postal Service from being an unwitting and unwilling drug courier. Even though it is helping pay the bills, they don't want your drug postage! Which is some bullshit because I know several people who order junk mail either because they want to have a large volume of mail or because they like helping out the postal service because it helps them out.

Postal inspectors use these criteria to identify packages that might contain drugs or other contraband:

* The package emits odors of marijuana or a masking agent (e.g., coffee, perfume, fabric-softener sheets)Don't do that. Always vacuum seal your weed at least three times. If possible use a heat sealed foil to top off the vacuum sealed plastic.

* The package is heavily taped along seams. Why does it need more than 1 layer of tape? Are you shipping water or something. This tells people your trying to seal in a smell.

* The package is poorly prepared for mailing. Make sure your items are snug inside the packaging and that if shaken you would not hear the contents moving around. Like pills in a container.

* The package or postage appears to have been re-used. Don't be a penny pincher. Especially don't use postage more than once if your shipping drugs.

* Has an uneven weight distribution. Only do this if your shipping a sledgehammer.

* The label Is handwritten. Don't you have a printer? It really looks like you were trying to avoid tracking of your package either through the internet or your computer might embed an identification when printing.

*   The label contains misspelled names, streets, or cities. Use a map fool! USPS knows to lookout for misspelled names going to your house. Why all of a sudden would your name be spelled a few letters off or a completely different name at your residence just starts receiving mail.

*   Originates from a drug source State. Stay away from Puerto Rico, Columbia, Huge boxes from California. Stuff like that.

*   Has been sent from an individual to an individual. This is usually ok as long as its not completely different

*   Contains return address ZIP code that does not match accepting post office ZIP code. This is usually ok as long it's the next town or city on the map. When you start skipping more than one post office to drop off your mail then there might be some suspicion.

*   Shows a fictitious return address. No ones going to believe LaLa Land Toy Company, Jointville California is a real place. This is simply solved by using a real return address with a business name. As long as the receiver doesn't use a suspicious name or address then there is no reason why it would be returned to sender.

*   Lists sender's and/or receiver's names of common type (e.g., John Smith) that are not connected to either

address. Of course use a fake name for the return address if you have to, just not the receiving address.

Those are some basic package receiving tips. They can also be used to ship product. Be smart and stay up to date on the latest techniques by visiting the forums and you will stay safe.

CHAPTER 2

THE MOST EXCITING, EXHILARATING, ADVENTUROUS MOMENT OF THE 2012 CALENDAR YEAR FOR ME!

The most exciting ,exhilarating, and adventurous moment of the 2012 calendar year for me was finally losing my virginity. My virginity to defy imagination and realize what is possible with technology that is. Who would have though that such a well thought out, secure, anonymous marketplace would pop up on the internet and allow people from all over the world to trade pretty much anything they want with each other.

It was just another day for me. I was off work from my miserable fast food job. In my spare time I enjoy smoking weed and flipping cannabis. Flipping cannabis makes my bills a little easier. Smoking cannabis makes me horny, hungry, and happy! Anyways I was simply chilling in my backyard, smoking some weed out of my glass mini bowl. Mine changes colors! Contemplating life while exhaling a lung full of smoke. I thought I was upset with where my life had gone. I had potential. The fact that I had caught several charges of the felonious nature as a teenager didn't help me at all in my plan to take all the worlds money by obtaining a nice job. It did qualify me for a minimum wage job at a local fast food restaurant. This in turn gave me some credibility to push some reefer while being white. I've always been a good salesman. I was currently reupping' on a quarter pound at a time. Yeah I said reupping, past tense of re-up. New word, no need to thank me. Now if my Microsoft word program would only add it to the dictionary I could stop tripping out because of all these red and green lines and how they are making me stop and stare at them. Because of the Nbome I recently ingested everything on the screen is moving, especially those red and green punctuation and spell check lines. Most of this book was written with a little help and motivation from my personal assortment of drugs. I bomb, you bomb, everybody n-bombs!

Focus. Ok, I'm back. The quarter pounds were mostly commercial although sometimes I would get hooked up with some lower spectrum mid for the same price. Some people I could only sell a quarter ounce to for $20 while others were more than ready to pay $6 a gram. I guess it depended on the situation and scarcity of bud in their lives. Either way I got it gone and was making decent coin for the little work I was doing. I had saved up enough money to purchase a pound but my dealer didn't want to do that. I couldn't blame him. I'd be skeptical about a white boy who sounded white moving shit so fast and wanting to buy some weight. I thought to myself: I'm not going to be able to increase my profit any more than what I currently have. Either I'm going to have to pull off a robbery or start selling addictive drugs. I thought about purchasing some hard because I knew one person to dump it off on but the legal consequences would far outweigh the benefits of the man's addiction I would reap. My life couldn't get any worse. Well it could but I figured my financial life couldn't. I went back inside to wash my hands and brush my teeth sad and depressed. You don't wash your hands and brush your teeth after smoking weed? It takes away some of the obvious tell-tale signs someone is stoned. Bud breath and bud fingers.

While I was in the process of reclining and flipping through channels, out of nowhere, a light bulb went off over my head. Was it a stroke of genius? Not it was not, apparently I had to run to my local Wal-Mart and buy some extra cfls because there wasn't any laying around the house and I didn't want to take one off the bathroom mirror to replace the one in the living room because I like to see how well the dandruff shampoo is doing on my itchy, dry scalp. After successfully driving to town and changing the bulb I booted up my then vulnerable

PC and entered the internet explorer browser which I would later know by the name: clearnet. I searched for get rich quick schemes. I was desperate ok. It's not like I'm a female and can call somebody to penetrate me for a few dollars. Upon reading several pages of articles and venturing past the first page of Google I stumbled across a comment where someone had a link to a certain Gawker article and claimed that if I read that then I would have a new insight into a great and seemingly safe way to get rich. All I can say is that as soon as I read that I thought it was some straight bullshit concocted by the DEA to obtain IP addresses of suspected/ potential drug dealers.

I've never been a gambling man but something told me to do a little more research and find out exactly what the Silk Road was all about. Sure enough I googled it and came across the version I was taught about in history class. Apparently you have to type 'marketplace' as well. Otherwise you're going to find the original Silk Road and not the new and improved version. Holy shit! This really seems too good to be true but at the same time I know that people with a great knowledge of computer systems can pull off a bunch of cool shit. Like those guys who hacked into the Wi-Fi of local restaurants to steal credit card information. This concept of buying drugs through the mail anonymously completely challenged my perception that you had to personally know somebody to score. I was stupefied, and excited enough that I almost came on myself just thinking about the possible possibilities of the adventure I could embark on and the buried treasure I was about to uncover.

I finally figured out how to place TOR on my Windows 7 operating system after a week of failed installation attempts. Then I had to search for a link to the hidden online Wal-Mart of drugs. That only took about an hour or two and I had to try two different web addresses. I managed to land on the basic looking login page where new members could register. I input no identifying information and wrote down my passphrase and PIN just like I do with my other legal website information until I am able to memorize it. Don't write yours down. If you do, memorize it and dispose of the evidence as quickly as possible. At first glance of the homepage I was hit in the face with a huge chunk of black tar heroin , what appeared to be a broken piece of kilogrammed cocaine, several LSD blotters and a few pics of some nice nuggetry of the dank kind. When I say hit in the face I mean like the featured items on eBay or other websites were on display. I knew then that whoever built this website was on top of their game to have pulled off this wonderful masterpiece of organized drug dealing. As I venture into my journey more I will uncover some more of the amazing thought processes that united to build this new kingdom of happiness that is able to cater to anyone, anywhere in the world where mail is able to be sent. Except maybe the middle east and China and shit places like that where the mail is probably opened and emptied of valuables before it is passed on to the recipient. I'm glad I live in

America, where laws protect you from being discovered by other laws, if that makes sense.

On the site itself, to the left of the page you can find more than a few categories of items drugs, electronics, digital goods, apparel, and even household just to name a few. I must admit it was a month of having access to the site before I even thought about looking at anything besides the drug section. No I'm not an addict; however drugs provide me with more of a financial incentive than cellphone jammers or the Thailand version of Red Bull. Although a signal jammer or a GPS tracking device can prove useful IRL if you ever needed to figure out when your local pot grower isn't home so you can raid for the cash and stash ;) Simply place the GPS tracker in their car or favorite shoes and wait for them to leave. No dude that wasn't me! Bring the money back you say? Hahahahahahahahaha… no. That never happened. It would be cool though if it did. Maybe when they make a movie about this book then they can do a scene where I use the GPS tracker to rob a grow house. I searched and checked out hundreds of listings for weed until I realized that I need to create a new account and select the United States as my home country and search for domestic products.

Now that I am able to only view domestic listings the search became a lot easier. It was just like real life where the price goes down as the weight goes up. The only drawback to this is that there is no way to organize listings by weight or quality.

An admin from the websites forums stated that this was to discourage competition. Which is perfectly fine with me and it keeps a lot more people in business. Just let me get right down to it though: There isn't really a point in paying for a single gram from somebody for $20 if they are going to charge $7 to ship it. I could get that delivered to me within the hour for cheaper for similar quality without risking a fucking postal inspector confiscating the overpriced bud. I don't think postal inspectors are bad people. I just don't like it when they try to take my drugs!!! The discounts came in at the ounce and quarter pound level(depending on the quality of weed you wished to purchase) all the way up to one pound listings. That would be pretty sweet to have the mailman drop a pound off on your porch and drive off none the wiser. I damn sure aren't going to order a pound to start off with. Even if I can get a decent looking one for $2500. So my search continues.

After having found a reasonably priced vendor who did not include pictures with his listings I did some research on him in the sites forum section. Apparently it's possible for location data to be extracted from pictures and erasing that data is a small task and to do that for every picture I imagine is somewhat of a time consuming process. Isn't it amazing what can be done with technology? I felt that the description was accurate and the listing even provided the name of the strain. Which I googled. That shit looked mouth wateringly delightful. I had to have it. Isn't it crazy that the technology that the military had a part in developing is now contributing to end the war on drugs in a civilized and brazen manner. Yes I used the word brazen silly politician, to describe the site and no I did not copy it from you, I googled it! To be bold and without shame is to behold my new role in the drug game!

So ecstatic was I about this hidden gem of technical know-how, and union of drug dealers. I can't even really describe it with words. I'm not even going to try. I would however like to thank the war on drugs for helping make this possible. If it wasn't for you then we would be free to ingest and purchase and distribute whatever substances we want to. Don't get me wrong I despise addictive substances and I think they should be kept in the hood! That came out wrong, I meant if you don't want the attention of law enforcement in your suburban neighborhood don't sell addictive substances and people won't be calling you at all hours or knocking on your door during your little brothers birthday gathering. Boy did that take some smooth talking to convince my mom not to call the cops. On the other hand I completely understand that if there isn't an addictive quality to some things then people will get tired and won't bother to steal some shit to make money to pay you for it. It's like the damn tobacco and alcohol companies, they are after profit yet kill the people that they sell to, and in some cases ruin their lives. Forgive me for my rant; I just don't like addictive substances.

By addictive I mean anything that has an elevated risk of physical and psychological dependency. Personally I think my girl should keep her legs shut because that shit keeps me coming back. No pun intended. Focus man focus. The war on drugs is to thank for the people imprisoned who have not caused harm to others. How the hell is it logical to punish someone for purchasing or possessing a little weed, or a few pills? If their intention wasn't to harm anybody then let them walk freely. The legal murderers and drug dealers are allowed to exist because they pay taxes and have possibly had an early start in influencing laws. If we stop supporting the tobacco and parts of the pharmaceutical companies who manufacture these addictive products then they will fail! I bet if people stopped buying cigarettes then pot would be legal and instead of tobacco fields there will be pot fields. I'm not saying weed is completely safe for your health, it is however a lot safer than tobacco and there is no risk of dependency. Give people a chance and stop feeding them poison for profit. I sell weed, LSD, and MDMA. The Lucy and Molly I make sure people understand some of the risks associated with it and I don't continue distributing it if I think someone is getting out of hand. Ask anybody I sell to. I am a very informative drug dealer and I got the sweetest shit in town. When pot is legal in my state you can bet ima be on top of that like DPR is on top of SR. DPR? Read the forums fool!!! Yes I went totally off topic in this chapter a little bit. I did however describe the moment of the year for me. Maybe if I didn't smoke so much weed I could actually remember stuff. Its all good though.

Here are some reefer quotes:

'Marijuana is socially unacceptable' says the country built on slavery.
-Unknown

For centuries marijuana has been used as a self prescribed remedy for the terminal disease known as 'being alive'
-Unknown

"'Is marijuana addictive?' Yes, in the sense that most of the really pleasant things in life are worth endlessly repeating."
-Richard Neville

God made pot. Man made beer. Who do you trust?
-Unknown

The connection has timed out

This is the end of chapter 2.

Please reload the page or consult the table of contents.

(That was a joke about connection timeouts! The book didn't get disconnected silly!)

CHAPTER 3

MY FIRST PACKAGE!!!!! BIGGEST SMILE EVER!!!!!!

The contents of my first package are confidential for security purposes! Yeah right. It was some weed fool! The strain and vendor on the other hand are confidential for security purposes. They might be reading this and realize who I am but I don't care because I used addresses besides my personal dwelling to receive packages. Get at me son!!! Just kidding dude, I loved the weed. I am offering a reward of 25 bitcoins to whoever can guess my real username. Here's how that is going to work. Someone will start a thread in the off-topic category and label it" Guess the Username of The guy Who Wrote: THE BOOK", then the first one to get it right without guessing will have some coins sent to their account. You can't tell anybody you got the coins. You can't create multiple accounts to keep guessing but I will also require that you have been an active forum poster when I was actually using the site. I will verify this by looking at some of your previous posts. Let the contest begin.

After figuring out how to get the online, digital, anonymous currency Bitcoins deposited into my account I had to put my plan into action. I skipped reupping that week to make a big purchase and risk it all. From what I could tell this online drug market was legit at being illegitimate and it would be safe for me to continue. I had a trusted friend setup a PO box for me in their name and they handed me off a key. If this is you then make sure your friend is TRUSTED completely and not simply trusted to a degree. A person who is trusted completely has never stolen from you and would never snitch your ass out. Hypothetically if this book was real then that would be considered mail fraud because they handed the key off to a user who wasn't reported when he signed up for the box. The only thing I had to do was bring him the skateboard catalogs and Hustler magazines, and of course the occasional Geico bills that would be sent there. I could only pick items up at night, although this would change as I got more comfortable with the stealth of my chosen vendors. I had bongs at my house that I wasn't going to get rid of. By doing this at night it enabled me to keep track of who was want to see what the difference powdered heroin provides over the black tar bullshit behind me. You never used headlights to see how long someone has been following you for? I don't know why I thought it mattered. My car damn sure couldn't outrun a police Interceptor. But do you know how much a ROOR costs? Enough to risk a high speed chase in the opposite direction of my house.

The plan was if something was to happen and when he was questioned about why there was drugs in his PO box then he would claim he lost the other key as it was kept in his wallet and that was stolen out of his book bag at lunch one day at the local community college. His house was clean and so was his computer. Looking back I still think it was a great setup. I know earlier I stated not to tell anybody but sometimes a partner is necessary if they can be trusted. Now to purchase the coin. I researched and decided on something. I damn sure wasn't about to go to a bank and make a deposit and handing my MoneyPak to a stranger on the website wasn't at the top of my to-do list. No I was lucky and still had access to bit instants cash deposit method. So here's how it went down: BI>MG>ZZ>wherever the fuck it goes after that>SR. Within an hour of making a cash deposit at my local location I had coins in my account. Only $800 worth. I do wish at the time I would have kept those because they were at the $11 range and at the start of me writing this book coins were worth $47. Fuck Wall Street. Buy coin! I should be the spokesperson for Bitcoin, Mt. Gox hit me up! Now what to do, what to do with all this money? I know. I found the item I wanted. I added it to my cart. I located the vendors Public PGP key. I copy and pasted that onto my computers

WordPad. I saved the file. I pulled up my PGP program and clicked import. I selected the vendors' key I had saved. I typed my address on the clipboard. I encrypted it. I copy and pasted the random mess of letters, numbers, and characters onto the address field of the sites checkout page. I entered my PIN. I am impatient so I am going to fast forward to the expected delivery day.>>Ok, I know that priority mail takes between 2-4 days to arrive but I decided to check on dia numero two! Not yet. Package is not here right now, please try again later. I wait another 24 hours before checking again and nothing yet. What the hell is going on? Oh so that's the difference between processing and in transit. Yeah I read the forums fool! Online drug dealers are very busy people and its not like they can just drop a baggie in a flat rate box, slap some postage on it and drop it off in one of the blue boxes. They have to actually get to your specific order as they are very busy people. Special care is required in ensuring a package of drugs arrives safely at its destination. The product has to be protected from smells leaking out.

This takes precision. It's not like you can just take a few ounces of loud, wrap it in dryer freshener sheets, throw it in the box, pour some coffee beans on it and expect it to work. A rolled joint of some dank stinks, a quarter pound absolutely reeks. I'm not going to disclose too much on the stealth of weed but as long as the outside of the package isn't suspicious enough to be opened then your in the clear. Its not like blotters which are easy to conceal in small items or paper-work. You definitely don't want to hollow out a peanut butter jar. Who the fuck ships peanut butter? The cost of shipping it would be equal to or greater than the price for which you can buy it in a store. Did you hear about the 10 pounds of weed that had a return address of a K-Mart store? It was returned for whatever reason(probably a bad 'to' address) and apparently had been wrapped in garbage bags and doused in some sort of fluid for smell protection. That's some stupid shit. Obviously the smell was contained or the postal employees involved in handling that particular package are stupid or just didn't care enough to report it. Hold on I need a bong break to get back on track to the current topic(chapter fool!). . . . .

Weed from the road is the bomb! It's exciting and potent and reasonably priced and it's very colorful. It was smooth hitting and the ashes were white. It wasn't trimmed all too well but it didn't affect it. That shit was great! I told my friends I had met a hippy from California who was on the run because the cops had busted his grow house which he operated without a medical card. They believed me too!

So today was the day! At least I hoped it was. Finally after weeks of anticipating this was not some scam by hackers or an attempt by LEO to zoom in on people I got off work one night and turned my cellphone off(read the forums fool!) and headed to the post office. I drove by one time in an attempt to spot any pig-mobiles! You know, the impalas, chargers, crown vics. Hell my county has an undercover civic and a taxi cab! Ya sneaky bastards! Pull me over if you want to I'm legit so I can talk shit and you can't really do too much about it except waste tax dollars investigating me because you think I am a drug dealer because I wrote this book. Silk Road is a hot topic and I'm surprised I'm the first one to write a book about it.

Anyways I pulled into the post office and made my way down the hallway of boxes wondering how many of those contained packages from the same website. I would later find out that the answer to that question was probably none as I had a monopoly on MDMA and Nbome in the surrounding counties as well as mine. I did not sell the Nbome as acid, however my resellers would on occasion. For drug safety tips visit bluelight forums or dancesafe! Made a hundred thou, from my mailbox! How ya like that Gucci? I'm very creative when I'm hyped up, hit me up dude! Ok advertisement over… on with the story. I attempt to insert the key but oops, I had it upside down. Reload. I insert the key again and twist the lock. I instantly felt this overwhelming feeling of excitement as I laid my eyes on the medium sized package. A feeling of joy rushed through my body. If I was on Dragon Ball Z my kai would be through the roof. This shit was real!

Why has the law enforcement community allowed this to continue? (Read the forums fool!) Hold up I'll save you some time. Basically, they can't! I lol'd as I walked out the door into the crisp night air. I had totally forgot about the cops and especially the police station one block up the street. I felt like Mr. Untouchable. You can't fuck with me was written on my forehead. I felt freer than those idiots who hijacked a helicopter to break out of prison. My mind was so clouded with pure happiness that I didn't wait to get home to open my bundle of joy and examine its contents. Like a kid sneaking a peek at his presents hidden in his moms closet a few weeks before Christmas I carefully opened the box to keep it intact in case I had to shove it under my seat. I reached into my pic-a-nic basket like Yogi Bear and snatched out a quarter pound of nuggetry. I couldn't tell that it was what was described in the items listing because of several layers of sneakiness. I undeniably couldn't smell anything but it didn't feel compressed at all which led me to believe the guy who sent it wanted me to be happy with its fluffy goodness. No one likes shake with their buds. Unless you were planning on making brownies to begin with.

We should ban shake in my opinion. Talk to your dealers and demand better treatment of your buds during handling and they will demand it to from their dealers, especially when you refuse to buy shakey ass weed. It was definitely better than the half ounce of shake I would sometimes get in my other quarter pound purchases from my non-internet supplier. Before I forget I must inform you that I never returned to the dealer I had before because of quality and price issues. He even left me voicemails a few times. Nothing bad except he was basically missing my business. Its lame when a dealer does cold calls. It's not like I forgot you, you dumbass. I just dropped you like a bad habit. Get over it. I hope you read this, and no I didn't have sex with her, I just threw some kaboshi down her throat. There was no reason for me to go back to my old, high priced for low grade weed dealer unless for some strange reason I needed commercial. The prices on the road for commercial weed are ridiculous. One time a guy was selling a quarter pound for 310. Come on dude ,IRL I was paying between 220-250. But to each his own.

OOOOOOOOOMMMMMMMMMGGGGGGG!!!
A cop car had gotten behind me and Im holding a quarter pound of high grade marijuana. I know I used my turn signals and stopped at the red lights completely, even though it had changed right as I stopped. My car lights are all working. My insurance and registration is up to date. It could only mean one thing… Oh wait he's just getting on the interstate. For a second I envisioned my new career over before it even began. I've got to get high, reliving these memories is causing a little bit of stress. First I will let you guys enjoy a poem I just thought of, yes its original.

I make it home

Safe and sound

In possession

Of a quarter pound!

That was pretty cool huh? Simple yet it really got the point across. Up the stairs I ran to my bedroom. I grabbed an over-sized mason jar I use to store my weed and empty out the little bit of commercial shake that is left onto my desk and make a neat pile for later use in my bowl. There is a huge difference in smell between commercial and high grade varieties. Yeah dude I'm smarter than the average pot smoking, pot selling bear. In a jar with a locking, rubber sealed lid there isn't going to be any detectable level of smell during a routine traffic stop. A whole case of varying sizes is available at your local Wal-Mart for under $20, so make an investment you potheads!

I couldn't rip open the packaging with my bare hands but luckily a pair of scissors was on hand and I was able to neatly cut away the first layer, then the second, then the third to reveal a gallon size Ziploc of some pretty beautiful cannabis. Upon cutting the second layer I couldn't help but notice a very nice, very strong, somewhat spicy aroma. At that point I had made up my mind about who I wanted to marry: Mary Jane. Her essence gave me hope. It filled my nostrils and my bedroom. It was like a skunk had blew up because it stepped on a landmine. I hurried and emptied the contents into three separate jars. It filled two and a half decent sized jars because like I said earlier, I could tell it was some fluffy stuffy. I snapped a pic of one of the bigger buds and it weighed out to 4.34 grams.

I daresay I got more than my money's worth because the next day when my mom wasn't home I opened a window and weighed it all out and to my amazement was over 4 grams. I could sell an ounce for a price that would thrash the prices of a native high grade dealer. If I did that some people might think I grew it myself, I always reply: No sir, my hippie runaway friend has a huge stash on deck. I can't even grow tomatoes! But usually I would keep it a steady $15 a gram, $160 for a half, $300 for a whole ounce. I already had a nice sized customer base and I would soon find myself going through a quarter pound every week.

This newly found mountain of drugs gave me hope. Hope that the few bills I had, car payment, car insurance, cellphone, fuel, food, rent whenever I could would be paid in a timely manner and I would still have plenty of money to spare on my girlfriend, backpage escorts(the pretty ones!) Chili's, bullshit from eBay and going ham on the electronics section at Wal-Mart. Hell I could even take sick days off at work and wouldn't even miss the $60 I would have earned that day minus taxes. Especially since it meant I wouldn't have to get in my car smelling like food. I hate fast food. I love money though. I guess that is why some people throw their lives into the brutality of the legal system to make an untaxed dollar. If no one is harmed by the crime then there should be no punishment. It appears to me that some people are so upset by the fact that someone got out of paying taxes that they are willing to write laws that imprison the tax evaders.

Rant Warning:

This is ridiculous as caffeine, tobacco, and alcohol companies are allowed to exist and push products that cause harm to not just the users but people around them. If you aren't into weed then you probably won't do it when it is legal. So why all the fuss? Cocaine used to be legal and I don't see why it shouldn't be now. Not the powder form that we know today but the leaves. I could see it now: it would be sold in packaging resembling Big League Chew. According to the Center for disease control and Prevention, smoking tobacco causes approximately 443,000 deaths per year. This accounts for nearly one in five of all deaths in the United States. More than AIDS, drugs, alcohol, car crashes, murder, and suicide combined. Yet its still legal and has no redeeming value. That sounds weird. It sounds like a schedule 1 drug to me. Only in America. I love this country yet hate it at the same time.

With all the common sense and street smarts available in my pot head, I thought it would be wise to destroy the package. I thought WWJD? He would set it on fire and send it to hell!!! And so did I. I ripped it into several pieces and threw it in the garbage bag. It was only half full but I figured I would just steal more from my workplace anyways. I went outside to the backyard and threw the bag of evidence into the fire pit. I ran back inside to grab a piece of newspaper and headed outside twisting the paper long ways into a hotdog looking thingy. I carefully placed it inside the opening of the trash bag and lit that bitch on fire. We always burn our trash and pack the ashes into garbage bags to save money and trips to the landfill which is about 9 miles away. It costs about .50 cents a bag so we figured why not.

This is a picture I took from a mobile device. I did not steal it from the internet or anybody else. I got to give credit. This is one of the many fine buds that await you on the Road. You probably cant tell the colors because I opted for the cheaper method of self-publishing this book. I will describe it for you: There is more purple than green on this one, It is dry, but not crunchy dry, the stench is absolutely tantalizing, the high is absolutely indicative of an indica. This of course isn't the best that's available but it is one of the best wholesale prices at about $175 a ounce.

I'm happy with my experience so far on the Road. The weed is moving great so in my mind it's time to invest in some other items. Next on the list is ecstasy!

CHAPTER 4

THE ROAD TO ROLLING!

Here is a great read! Seriously read over it. This chapter will describe some of my experiences receiving and selling and of course using MDMA. It will also go over some excellent safety tips regarding the use of MDMA that will make your overall ecstasy experience a better one.

Now that you have had a chance to get acquainted to the Road and how to properly use it I will inform you guys of some of my experiences with "Love". The thing with ecstasy is that if you wish to purchase a lot to resell then you will most likely have to venture outside of the domestic U.S. vendors. A lot of the US vendors on the site actually buy from overseas Silk Road Vendors. To order high quality MDMA at a decent price you will definitely have to do this. The only exception would be to purchase a lot of methylone. It is a similar high at a much cheaper cost. There are a few differences between the two. If you have taken both then you already know what they are. Just don't be an asshole and purchase the cheap shit just to resell it as 'Molly'. It's not the same thing. It is possible for you to sell a metric shit ton of methylone in a short time to acquire funds to purchase a bulk quantity of the real deal, either in pill or powder form. That's what I did☺. It worked out great to. I easily quadrupled my money to end users and doubled it by selling to resellers. I finally saved enough to risk purchasing 1 kilo of it but at about $6500 you can't beat it. End users still got the $70 a gram price while I lowered the price to my resellers to $40 a gram. That's how I ended my Road addiction. I retired from it.

On to the story. It started out like any normal Friday afternoon. I entered the cold, scary hallway of my local Post Office. Scary because every time I go into one of these storage sheds for drugs I always have the popo at the back of my mind. Ready to throw me down as soon as I pick up my package and start walking out the door. Luckily for me I had chosen a quality vendor who knows what it takes to get a package through to the end user. I pulled the color coded key out of my pocket and penetrated the law by opening the door that separated me and this seemingly harmless package which contained several x-pills. I had several PO boxes for deliverys setup and the sharpie the po uses to mark the number on it always wipes off so I used several different masking tapes in alphabetical order to help me identify which key I needed to bring from home.

At the time I wasn't sure of what was exactly in the package but I had a pretty good idea. I have been lucky and never had a vendor not send me something as described. I exited one of the few government buildings I don't have negative thoughts about and got into my car. I looked over my shoulder and backed out of the space and pulled off towards the exit. I felt pretty good about this one being a safe pickup and opened the package. It wasn't to complicated the find the small sample container of two "high quality" MDMA pressed tablets. They looked like the x-pills I was used to getting from a friend back in 2007. There was only one way to find out. I used to just pop them into my mouth and grind them up with my teeth because I couldn't wait for that shit to start kicking in. Instead I pulled into one of the local drive thru snack and beverage shops, purchased a mango flavored Snapple, handed a five dollar bill to a longtime friend of mine who works there as well as the other pill. We were cool like that and it was almost time for him to get off work anyways so get over it. I didn't have any qualms about handing one out because of safety issues that it might be something other than ecstasy. I simply remembered this little fact: I bought it from an underground drug website that incorporates a feedback system to ensure product quality and weed out scammers. If you do your research on the site and the vendor you want to purchase from you will almost always get what was advertised.

Driving off and out of the parking lot I cracked that top and learned a fun-fact, drowned the pill and my taste buds, and put that top right back on. About an hour later I was able to confirm the authenticity of the tablet. This rush of happiness and sweatiness had filled my pores. I needed some pussy. My girl was at work and wouldn't be home until the end of my roll. Bad timing on my part but whatever. I'll simply order some prostitutes. Dammit the road doesn't sell that! Plan B… COD!!!! I love COD. Raise your hand if you do too. My username is *********-****. Hit me up so I can kick your ass on Nuketown. Dude you actually typed that in? Don't you just hate censorship? Of course I'm not going to tell you my real COD username.

I am feeling really great right now. This t-shirt is coming off. Its 71 degrees on my thermostat and 63 outside but in my room it feels like the fucking sun almost. Popped a molly and my body begins its cool down phase! I love ecstasy. I only wish I had someone to talk to. I didn't have a Bluetooth for my Ps3 and I didn't really feel like conversing with the online gaming community anyways. Its 11am usually that time of day the adult gamers are still sleeping and the kids who skipped school that day are online and cussing like sailors. Don't you just hate that? You get on to enjoy a nice game of Team death match and out of nowhere a munschkin nube-toobs you, ending your kill streak. A verbal assault follows, and you just want to beat the shit out of the kid because of it. I don't care if you're a midget at that point, if you talk shit about someone's mother you have just given them permission to physically confront you. The nerve of some of these kids.

I've never been a talker. I illustrate thoughts with action. Fuck the bullshit ya feel me?

Its not even a challenge anymore. At one point I held the #1704 spot on the Black Ops leaderboard. I bullshit you not. Fast fingers is what they called me. Or would've called me that if someone had thought to describe my finger movements. Oh what a boring day this is turning out to be.

Chores have to be done and ecstasy is a great motivating factor for anybody who has chores to be done. You should try it sometime and see how much you can get accomplished when you've put some pep in your step. I have pit bulls. I love pit bulls period. They stink. Not bad but I usually only wash them every two weeks. Today is definitely bath day. Some might laugh at what I'm about to describe but I'd like to see you wash them another way without getting bit. I tried tying them on the porch and using a hosepipe but I'd rather be one of the pit-bull owners where he doesn't get mauled by his own dogs.

I start by rounding all three of them up in the bathroom. This may sound ludicrous to some but they love each other so this is never an issue. I throw some swimming trunks and water shoes on. I grab the dog shampoo and remove every other item from the bathtub(bars of soap, shampoo bottles, razors,etc) This is so they don't make a big mess by knocking stuff out of the bathtub with their crazy, powerful tails. I then turn on the water until it gets about as hot as a baby human would be comfortable with. I'm not going to spray my dogs with cold water, they don't like that shit! Trust me. I then attempt to verbally call one into the tub with me. They know commands but they don't like the shower so this only works about 10% of the time. Simply grab one by the collar and drag them in with me. Next, close the curtain and turn the water back on and massage all the excess dirt out and make sure they are soaked. Turn the water back off(water conservation!) and lather them up real good for about 4-5 minutes. The last step is to turn the water back on and rinse them really good. I wish I had a removable shower wand but this is not the case. Instead I have to stand them up on their hind legs while the water is running to rinse the belly. I lied, the last step is to grab a towel and dry them off as much as possible before letting them out of the tub.

Once all my wittle wuppys have been cleaned it's time to clean the bathroom floor and bathtub. I recommend Scrubbing Bubbles and Mr Clean brand products. That was easy and my dogs are happier than before. I think they get happier everyday. You just gotta show them some love and never treat them like shit and they will always be good to you. It doesn't make sense for anyone to let their dog become a "bad" dog. The only thing some pitbull owners might have trouble with is other animals. These dogs were bred to fight. I have had a few. The ones I received which had papers usually were better able to control their obvious hatred of any other creature with four legs. The ones I had bought from irresponsible owners usually meant that the dogs parents hadn't been raised in as much of a loving environment as their registered counterparts. It makes sense. Which is why I will only support shelter dogs and registered dogs from now on.

Alrighty, what next do I have planned for today? I don't really remember. Did I have plans? Wait a second I gotta phone call. " Yo"..."probably like 30 minutes"..."later". Get your shoes on I gotta delivery to make. First I need to shower up because I smell like wet dog and flea shampoo.

Grab one of my scales because I got some weighing to do! A good drug dealer keeps a few different scales on deck. For bulk weed I have a .0, for smaller quantities of weed like single grams I have a .00, and for powder or crystals I have a .000. All this shit I bought off of eBay for very good prices. My local head shop wanted $180 for a .000 I got from eBay for $60, shipping included. I have no use as of yet for the .000 but I plan on ordering a lot of MDMA in its pure form in the near future.

Today I would need the .0. For some reason I felt in a hurry and that it had to be done to save time but I was fresh out the shower I dried off and dropped the towel and ran down the hall and up the stairs naked to my room. I grabbed a few baggies out of my baggie drawer and one of my cannabis containing jars out of another. The scale always sat on my desk.

I needed two ounces. It took about 5 separate weighing's but I got it all in the bags. The tray with a raised edge that came with the scale will hold about 16 grams before you really have to start playing Jenga with it. I usually just throw a half on it at a time, throw it in the bag, repeat. I insist that my resellers have their own jars for the weed and the drop point isn't too suspicious so I don't mind riding through town with the inside of my car smelling like a greenhouse.

It's off to the local Wal-Mart to pick up a black guy. No you can't buy a black guy at Wal-Mart. Maybe at White-Mart. No, no, I seriously meant I was picking up a black guy. Not buying one. It goes down like this at Wal-Mart. I never leave my car. Ever. Usually someone will already have had a ride drop them off and they are just standing around smoking a cig. Might go inside and buy some candy and a drink or something. Go out front and wait to be picked up by me. Hop in and hand over the cash, I hand over the stash and it goes straight into their jar. I don't need to count and they don't need to weigh because my shits always on point, always. Besides why the fuck would you want to mess up a great weed dealer like me by not having all the cash? That'd be stupid on someone's part. It never happens.

Anyways, we then head up the street to a local fast food restaurant. They exit the vehicle and enter their ride that is already waiting and we part ways. Simple as that, there is no need for sketchy looking handshakes or the usual " check out my "subwoofer and amplifier in the trunk dude!" Anyways I'm sweating and I need a fucking milkshake or something. Vendor wasn't kidding when he said 310mg. I guess that would be considered a triple stack. That's another thing I hate too. How much drug, is in a stack? Like seriously? Do you know what a stack equals too? Someone not knowing how much that pill contains is what a stack means.

I love the road because drug dealers on there are for the most part honest about doses and use proper terms and not slang. Legalize it, it's a life saver! Just think about it: a method of purchasing drugs that doesn't involve face to face real world transactions. Do you know how much safer it would be for the users as well as the police. If you stumbled upon my several thousand dollar drug deal your probably getting lit up donut boy. But they can't do that if the transaction takes place in your mailbox now can they?

Time for my next shipment. Well what the fuck happened to the rest of your day with the first pill you ask? Um, I went home and just smoked some more weed and thought about how bad of an idea it was to take the damn thing and not have access to vagina until the pill wore off. That's why. No my next order would prove to be far more fun. I placed an order for 100 grams of methylone. I figured I could easily buy some gelatin capsules online and a .000 scale and make my own "Molly". It wasn't often that I came across the brown stuff in capsules in my town, and when it is available its extremely pricey. It's like $30 for a capsule that contains close to .250 grams. This was an opening I immediately realized I could exploit.

I make the trip to my local deposit location. On the way there I simply used bitinstant.com to setup the amount and did everything from my smartphone. I didn't think it wouldn't look suspicious if I used TOR to do it so I might as well do it in the car. The amount I was attempting to purchase required three separate deposits. I probably could have done it all in one day but I settled for two. The old Bitinstant method usually had coins in my account in under two hrs so I simply placed an order for one, waited til it was deposited and visited the other deposit location under a different name and information and made the second deposit. The only thing I had to remember to do was refresh my bitcoin address on the site. This ensures I didn't get caught up in any type of fraud alert system.

So all my coins are in place, it's time to order some money!!! I plugin the battery to my laptop. I keep it separate so it would make it that much harder for someone to attempt to use it. I got mine from the Road itself. Its encrypted and only cost about $1000. They took a basic Lenovo Thinkpad. The one with the finger print scanner. Encrypted it to the max with several layers of protection and sent it to my mailbox. I of course had to pick mine up out of the larger ones. You know where they leave a special key for the huge mailboxes in case you get something that won't fit in yours. I love my drug dealing laptop. Its much better than my old Presario in terms of protection. You should invest in one.

Scrolling through the MDMA listings I realize the purer stuff is a lot more expensive so I definitely am going to go with the methylone. I find one of several vendors that sell the cheap ecstasy. They usually sell it in 1, 5, 14, 28, 50, 75, 100, 250, and 1000 gram listings. The price drops on each one but I only had enough for the 100 gram listing. Which was fine for me because it only costs about $1100 and I figured I could easily make $50 a gram on it. Dropped the methylone in my shopping cart and checked out using PGP.

Now the waiting game begins. It wasn't like weed. If you got caught with this shit they would consider it ecstasy. Even though it's really ecstasy's little sister. That definitely would equal some serious jail time in my state. Hopefully my vendor knows what he/she is doing when they drop mine off in the mail. It would probably be a shootout if I could pull my pistol out fast enough on any cop that attempted to not let me walk away from the situation. I'd rather be dead than die in jail. If someone gets a life sentence I think it should be an option to die by lethal injection. This would save me years of wasting my life anyways and it would save the state years of wasted funds. That's just my .02 on the subject.

The days pass by and I continue to receive two more packages of weed. One is right in the next town. They haven't caught on to those yet. Maybe this one will make it through. It will definitely be more profit than the weed. It has to make it through.

I think today is the day. Ima be cautious though and scope out the situation. I arrive on the street the post office is on about 11pm at night. I drive by once just to check for any cops actually sitting in the parking lot, none. I bust a left at the light and drive a little ways down the street checking out the few parked cars and checking out the driveway to see if one actually pulled in and parked there. I drive around the block to end up back in front of the post office and checked out the street to the right of the stoplight this time. Sure enough it seemed like I was in the clear. I decided to pull into the post office and pull up onto the curb. This would give me a little advantage if I decided to make a quick escape. With my key ready before I got out of the car I headed inside. Opened my special drug delivery box and to my amazement it simply looked like someone had sent me something not suspicious. I quickly threw the envelope into my pants and pulled out a letter from a company that attempts to make you purchase an extended warranty for your car. Don't you just hate those?

The point of me stuffing the envelope down my trousers and pulling out the decoy letter was to make it look like I had used a different PO Box which is why I came out with something other than the package of ecstasy. It was smooth how I did it too and the way the Post Office interior is designed is that you would have had to be inside to see that I did it. I felt so happy, so amazed that someone had actually taken the time out of their day to send me drugs in the mail. I've got to hurry home and finalize the payment for this kind stranger. Did I forget to mention the site uses an escrow system to make sure the buyer gets what they pay for. Who would've thought that a site that sells drugs would have something like this.

On my journey home I don't even bother looking at it. I know in my mind it is there. Im still a little worried about getting pulled over so I open the package to confirm there isn't a GPS device inside. Sure enough there wasn't. I could feel through the vacuum sealed package of powder that there wasn't.

Finally home so its time to experiment. I mean I couldn't just start selling this shit without having tried it first. I've read plenty about it so I have a good idea of what to expect but just to make sure. I pulled out my .000 scale and calibrated it. The next step involved figuring out how to get the powder into the tiny gelatin capsule. After careful thought and consideration I decided to use a medicine dropper with the rubber end removed. I would the take a piece of card paper from a medicine box and roll it into a funnel and insert the funnel into the dropper.

Holy shit that was a great idea. The only other modification I had to make was to cut a little off of the dropper end to ensure I had a seamless flow of powder into the capsule. I made a perfect cut and it stuck right into the end of the capsule. I simply was able to rest the capsule on one of my fingers, insert the dropper end and pour a predetermined amount of powder into the funnel. I would give the dropper a flick of my finger a few times to make sure I got most of it. Simply remove the dropper and pop the top of the capsule back on and you have successfully made your first methylone cap!!!

I weighed out .150 grams to take for my first time. I licked my fingertips after weighing my test capsule out and guess what? It tastes like shit. I don't recommend anyone eat this or snort it. Use the cap. And next time I will acquire some latex gloves to do the capping with. I really don't want my fingers getting high.

So its about 45 minutes ago that I ingested the cap on an empty stomach. I'm starting to get that alert feeling. The feeling you get as you start to come up on something. If someone had ingested the cap unknowingly and never done drugs before they would be feeling pretty weird about now. They might even call a doctor. But everything will turn out alright. Don't worry.

It's about an hour in now and I'm starting to sweat and I definitely want to start talking to somebody. It's time to visit the local Hooters restaurant. I know Ima look funny as hell walking in about 30 minutes before closing time by myself but I didn't care. I'm feeling great right now and no one is going to put a damper on my night. I go in and sit down. Scantily clad 18 and 19 year olds were starting to sweep up. Maybe this was a bad idea in me coming here. For the first time in my life I felt like a rapist watching his prey. Snap out of it man here she comes!

A brunette came up and asked me how I was doing. All I could do was smile, I smiled hugely. "I'm doing exceptionally well" I said in my best British accent. I have no clue why I did that but I did. When I get geeked up on something I turn into this charismatic, funnier than usual, anti-Johnny Blazed. "Are you really British or are you just messing around?" said the Hooters girl. With a serious look on my face" Of course I'm British, what ta ell kinda question is that?" . Holy shit Im having too much fun. I had totally lowered my expectations about how powerful a roll this methylone would be. Everybody says it sucked compared to the original MDMA. This shit is pretty cool and for the price you can't fuck with it." Just run along an get me some water and some sweet tea please" . My wish was done and she actually asked me could she take my order." What, you can tell a British guy when you see one but you can't see that I want some fish and chips?" "sir we don't have that, I'm so sorry would you care for anything else?""No thank you but I would like my check please. This has been a rather unpleasant experience for me." I said in an even better British accent than before. I needed to get out of there before someone called the cops. It was obvious to me that it was obvious to my waitress that something was wrong with me.

Back outside in the cool night air I felt alive. Like a natural aspirated car engine inhaling more compressed oxygen in the late fall, I felt more powerful than ever. (If I was on Dragon Ball Z my kai would be through the roof.) I felt like a super saiyan. I hopped in my ride and turned it to the local hip hop station. R I P I just killed the Hooters! Ha-ha that was a good one. Yes I think I will turn the volume up a little bit more this song is catchy. I really shouldn't be driving but the only problem I've ever had while driving would be that I sometimes lose my sense of direction and have to think about where I'm going.

Hell I remember the first time I smoked weed and drove. We were in the car just laughing and joking, especially when I stopped at two greenlights. That was pretty stupid. Luckily we didn't get pulled over. It was some good times back in the day though. I wish I was in Peter Pan land and I could never grow up. Oh well, I guess I'll have to wait until somebody invents a time machine. If I am able to venture back in time I would go back and change things, like I would have actually paid attention in school and stayed out of trouble. I would definitely stay away fro The Silk Road. The amount of trouble I could easily get into isn't even funny. There should be some kind of limit to the amount of drugs I can purchase in a given time period.

"At the same time it is a good thing that I can order any drug I want. That good thing is freedom. Freedom to do what I want, as long as I'm not harming others. If I choose to ingest drugs then let me. If someone chooses to ingest drugs then let them. It's not your money being spent. I can't tell you not to smoke tobacco or drink alcohol. So what gives you the right to tell me I can't smoke pot or drink some mushroom tea."

"We were all created equal according to mortal men and GOD himself. So what the fuck is your problem." Holy shit I'm looking at a picture of Uncle Sam on my phone for some reason. That was pretty weird. What's even weirder is that I just pulled into a gas station when my car has three fourths of a tank left. I need to hurry and get home.

So I make it home, safe and sound. Oh you thought it was going to be another poem didn't ya? Ill consider writing a few more and putting them in the book somewhere. I go up to my bed and cuddle next to my girlfriend. I didn't really feel like having sex and I wasn't going to wake her up because she has to work in the morning. Aren't I a nice and respectful guy? I felt more like cuddling anyways. This wasn't exactly like the ecstasy pills I was used to. It was definitely worth the money though.

I felt like cuddling anyways. No I'm not a pussy. Girls happen like that stuff when a man is not focusing on his own penis' intentions and caters to her need to feel good. I do to. Especially when I'm rolling. Feeling her body heat and soft skin is very relaxing. You should try it sometime.

I later fall asleep a short while later. In the morning when I wake up and I feel like shit. That usually happens the day after a roll. When I wrote this book I came across possible reasons why I feel like shit the day after a roll. That information is below. Please use it. It has definitely had a positive effect on my other rolls I have had since writing this chapter.

Here are some safety tips regarding the use of MDMA (ecstasy) It would be wise for you to follow these guidelines for having safe ecstasy experiences. MDMA releases then depletes serotonin in vast amounts and inhibits the enzyme responsible for producing more serotonin, tryptophan hydroxylase (TPH). The inhibition is permanent, so the body must compensate by creating more and this restoration typically takes 1-3 months. Taking MDMA prior to this restoration process is altogether stupid. Your body's reproduction of serotonin is already inhibited and by taking the substance during this healing period will start the entire process over.

MDMA work as follows:

MDMA binds to the SERT and reverses it causing a dump of serotonin. The hypothalamus directs the release of cortisol (an 800% increase) and ADH as a defense response to combat the serotonin release. This increases the speed at which serotonin is metabolized in the brain.

This is the "come-up." A sharp spike in serotonin characterized by a rise in cortisol levels. Skyrocketing cortisol levels are responsible for the come-up anxiety many users describe. And the rise in serotonin can sometimes cause nausea or bowel problems. Next: Serotonin is an inhibitor of dopamine in 3 out of 4 pathways. The brain-wide rise in serotonin levels is clogging up dopamine pathways and causing a buildup. Serotonin and cortisol levels both spike and begin to fall. When serotonin drops, the dopamine pathways open up and a rush of dopamine is released. Imagine a dam breaking. And with the rush of dopamine comes a release of oxytocin and prolactin into the bloodstream a la the hypothalamus. This is the peak of MDMA. Characterized by a fall in serotonin and a rush of dopamine in the mesolimbic pathway. The part that separates MDMA into its own category of fun is the systematic release of dopamine, prolactin, and oxytocin, not serotonin.

Dosing also plays a very large part in MDMA neurotoxicity as well, as it scales exponentially the more you take at a given time. With higher doses you are prone to hyperthermia and a decrease in antioxidant levels to deal with metabolites. While we lack the quantitative data for measuring the true damage done to a human due to obvious reasons, the neurotoxicity is very well established within mice and rats (see footnotes) and caution should be taken when choosing how much MDMA to ingest (1.5mg/Kg, more on that below).

While the choice to roll often is obviously at the user's discretion, the best experience is had by maintaining this healthy time frame and also following a few general guidelines.

Keep your body temperature low, don't overdo it by feeling pumped and think you can dance or have sex all night without a break! Ensure that you do not overexert yourself when dancing as an increase in body temperature is the leading cause of MDMA induced neurotoxicity. As your body temperature rises, your body's natural process for creating antioxidants is negatively affected and oxidative stress is increased, which leads to damage to your 5-HT axons. Take plenty of breaks when dancing so that you maintain a low body temperature.

Eat right and exercise. This is a no-brainer. The healthier you are, the better your body will be able metabolize MDMA. You shouldn't be wasting your money on drugs if you are fat and out of shape anyways, call Jenny or get a gym membership and eat right.

Enjoy MDMA for what it is and don't utilize it to get intoxicated. It is meant to bring about an incredible experience that should be limited to once every two to three months. MDMA for me at least gives me an almost everlasting boner, it provides me with a profound outlook on life as a whole. I open up my true

Know your dose and do not re-dose! The general rule of thumb for dosing pure MDMA is 1.5mg/Kg. Given you have no tolerance, this is an excellent guideline and should be practiced thoroughly. If need be, take a booster (typically half of your initial dose) no later than an hour to an hour and a half after the initial dose. It might seem fun to get straight geeked the fuck up but in reality your body is suffering any subsequent doses will only greatly increase neurotoxicity and make the negative effects much more profound. Pre-load, post-load! Pre-load, post-load! Just like a bodybuilder! This is CRITICAL and there is no reason not to do this as the vitamins are cheap and very effective. Antioxidants prior to your roll will largely alleviate neurotoxicity. Vitamin C, Vitamin E, Co-Q10, Alpha Lipoic Acid are all phenomenal antioxidants. A few other notables to smooth out your roll are magnesium glycinate for bruxism (jaw clenching) that weird feeling you get where you feel like you can't help but grind your teeth. I never get nauseated but I usually fire up some OGK or you can use ginger root for nausea. It is typically advised to take these one hour prior to ingesting the MDMA/ecstasy. If available, taking an SSRI on your comedown is very beneficial as it will prevent the uptake of nasty metabolites. A multivitamin at the end of your roll is also beneficial. Even though you won't want teat you need to EAT! Eat lots of food. Fill your overheated, drugged out body with nutrients. You just exhausted your mind and body and it needs to refuel! Soups, fruits, and vegetables are great for the comedown and light on the stomach. Stay hydrated but don't overdo it. Gatorade is pretty handy.

This is a no-brainer, but it still needs to be reiterated. Drink a reasonable amount of water to compensate for whatever activity you're participating in, especially if you're dancing. Dehydration is not a state you wish to find yourself in. It's not a state like California but rather a state that usually somehow involves you ending up in the hospital.

Here are a few articles on the internet which will provide you with more information on MDMA and cover most if not all of what I have told you already about MDMA. I urge you to visit these and share this knowledge with others. You might sound like a dork but at the same time you are possibly saving someones life so grow some balls and be an informative drug dealer!

On neurotoxicity:

http://dancesafe.org/drug-information/ecstasy-and-neurotoxicity
http://www.erowid.org/references/refs_view.php?ID=750
http://jop.sagepub.com/content/24/2/175

On supplements/SSRIs:

http://www.ncbi.nlm.nih.gov/pubmed/10619665
http://www.ncbi.nlm.nih.gov/pubmed/2433425
http://www.erowid.org/chemicals/mdma/mdma_article3.shtml
http://www.neurosoup.com/schedule1/mdmamainpage.htm

And of course, the main erowid MDMA page will inform you have read!

http://www.erowid.org/chemicals/mdma/

Here is some bkMDMA (methylone) This little bit could easily be sold for a few thousand dollars just wholesaling it $40 a gram. This was taken from my mobile device and I own all rights to this picture.

CHAPTER 5

GET YOUR BITCOIN ON!

In this chapter I will go over some of the techniques I used to obtain coins, what are bitcoins, and some interesting information about the usage of bitcoins. It may or may not be in that order, I don't really know yet ok? Now what was I talking about. Oh wait, bitcoins got it. Ok according to Wikipedia:

Bitcoin (sign: BTC) is a decentralized digital currency based on an open-source, peer-to-peer internet protocol. It was introduced by a pseudonymous developer named Satoshi Nakamoto in 2009.

The Bitcoin logo is easy to identify. It is basically a capital B with two lines running through the middle. Picture a dollar sign $ instead of one line it has two and instead of the S it has a B.

Internationally, bitcoins can be exchanged by personal computer directly through a wallet file or a website without an intermediate financial feelings to people, sometimes this is a bad thing but it really helps me get points across sometimes. Applying Self-control is a big part of the ecstasy experience as it is so much fun to do you will want to skip the recovery period. Learn to resist the urge to take it, especially when under the influence of alcohol. The two really should NOT be combined. Why would you want to do it with anything other than weed or orange juice anyways?

institution. In trade, one bitcoin is subdivided into 100 million smaller units called satoshis, defined by eight decimal places.

Bitcoin does not operate like typical currencies: it has no central bank and it solely relies on an internet-based peer-to-peer network. The money supply is automated, limited, divided and scheduled, and given to servers or "bitcoin miners" that verify bitcoin transactions and add them to an archived transaction log every 10 minutes. The log is authenticated by ECDSA digital signatures and verified by the intense process of brute forcing SHA256 hash functions of varying difficulty by competing "bitcoin miners." Transaction fees may apply to new transactions depending on the strain put on the network's resources. Each 10-minute portion or "block" of the transaction log has an assigned money supply. The amount per block depends on how long the network has been running. Currently, 25 bitcoins are generated with every 10-minute block. This will be halved to 12.5 BTC during the year 2017 and halved continuously every 4 years after until a hard limit of 21 million bitcoins is reached during the year 2140.

Bitcoin is the most widely used alternative currency. As of March 2013, the monetary base of bitcoin is valued at over $600 million USD. The large fluctuation in the dollar value of a bitcoin has evoked criticism of bitcoins economic suitability as a currency.

Wow, an entirely digital currency that can be used worldwide! Not that everybody uses this as a form of payment. I wouldn't load up your bitcoin wallet and catch an intercontinental flight and hope the town you land in accepts this as payment. It is however becoming increasingly popular and one day in the future you could just walk into a store and pay for an item simply by sending coins to the stores address.

For now however it is an excellent investment. When I first started using the Road bitcoins were valued at about $11 USD for just one bitcoin! Upon writing this chapter they are now worth $72 a piece! I have a few stocked up and they have gained considerable value if I chose to sell them. I think I'll hang on because I read an article on the web stating that the value of a bitcoin could potentially reach a few thousand dollars. That is very exciting.

The only thing that concerns me is that if everybody's money is tied up in bitcoins as the only currency then it is possible for us all to be royally screwed if the electricity went out. There would be no way to verify how many coins somebody had. That would be horrible. We need to keep several currencies at our disposal. Some physical such as the dollar, gold, silver and other precious metals, as well as digital currencies, such as bitcoin!

How many people think bitcoin is a part of the N.W.O plan to control the world? If we don't come to rely on methods that have no backup plan then we will not fall victim. Keeping our guns is just as important as keeping reliable methods of bartering at our disposal. Bitcoin is not a bad thing. I think it should simply be treated as an investment and buying drugs is a great investment! Well if you have a great deal, obviously for drugs to be a great investment you would probably need to buy more than a personal supply.

Or you could buy some bitcoins now and wait until I release this book! It's called speculation and those old white fuckers on Wall street are to blame. Of course I am already somewhat familiar with paying for something and waiting awhile to sell it. I am currently invested in the newly emerging medical marijuana industry. I could sell all my coins or all of my stock now but I think I'm going to wait a few more years and watch it grow before my eyes. Like a baby to a kid to a teen to an adult my money will grow. Now is definitely time to buy though. Like I said before, the coins are potentially going to be worth thousands of dollars, especially as they become increasingly rare due to their original, intended design.

There are several methods of obtaining bitcoins. The first would be to join a bitcoin exchange site such as Mt. Gox. The only problem with this is that they usually require identification. Bitcoins are legal though right? Yes, unless you are using them to buy drugs. If you got busted and forgot to encrypt your computer then it is possible for law enforcement to see that you visited the bitcoin exchange site as well as an online marketplace for drugs. You could then be charged with some form of money laundering because they are able to prove that you purchased the bitcoins specifically for the purpose of buying drugs. If you were able to purchase bitcoins somewhat anonymously and have them sent to your account on the site then it would be next to impossible for law enforcement to say that you ordered the package they intercepted because you purchased the coins as well.

Another one that I have used would be the cash deposit method. You simply locate a site that turns cash deposits into bitcoins. It usually works like this: At a time when bitinstant. com was functional you simply typed information onto a page of the website indicating how much money you would like to deposit and how you would like to deposit it. It would also ask for some identifying information but I always chose a fake name and address and telephone number. You would then submit the information and it would provide you with instructions on where to go to make a cash deposit. The most popular method was filling out a blue MoneyGram form. If this was done at your local Wal-Mart then you can deposit up to $1000 at a time. Places like CVS and gas stations usually have a $500 limit. You simply walk inside and fill out the MoneyGram form with the fake information you provided to the website and pay the cashier the deposit plus whatever fee the website charges and that was it! A few hours later you will have bitcoins in the bitcoin address you provided to the website.

One of the most private ways however is to use the website itself but can potentially be a ripoff or scam if you don't research your vendor by inquiring about recent buying experiences with the vendor in question. You simply logon and visit the Money category. You will find vendors are buying and selling bitcoins in exchange for cash in the mail or prepaid money cards. I'm not going to divulge too much of this information as my methods may be outdated. You will have to check the website forums for the safest, up to date methods.

It is possible to find local people selling bitcoins. Simply do a web search for local bitcoin sellers and you will find several websites where people are more than happy to buy or sell you coins. These websites often require some contact with the other person. They are probably in the same boat as you are so I don't think it would be too much of a hassle if you don't mind being friendly for a few minutes to see that your coins are moving through the block chain.

Wait!!! I'm not done yet. You need to visit one of several bitcoin gambling websites where it is possible to place bets with bitcoins in the hopes of winning bitcoins. Just be smart and don't use all your coins on these places. If you have a gambling problem please call on of several gambling hotlines. I wouldn't mention bitcoin though or your exact location and personal information.

CHAPTER **6**

A CHAPTER I WILL ATTEMPT TO TYPE ENTIRELY TRIPPING ON LSD (THE ORIGINAL ACID!)

Everybody has heard about it but few young people today have actually had the opportunity to experience it. By it I mean LSD(acid, Lucy) You may have had something on a blotter tab that made you have a very different trippy experience but it probably wasn't real LSD like the dealer said. What do you mean Johnny? I'm saying that you were probably sold a new research chemical that was designed to mimic the effects of real LSD. It is very possible that this has happened to you.

Many new research chemicals are placed on blotter tabs. Blotter tabs are thought of to contain LSD as this was the most popular method of distributing LSD. Some people think it is ok to sell blotters with research chemicals as LSD. This is not ok.

This is 25i-Nbome:

This is a sheet (900) hits of 25i-Nbome. This picture was taken from my mobile device.

Do you see how easily someone could substitute the 25i in place of the LSD in the blotter? There are a few ways to tell them apart aside from being a guinea pig. There is a notice-able difference in price and the way the product is used which should make you realize which is which, if you encounter someone selling blotters claiming that they are "acid". The old saying goes if it's a bitter it's a spitter. Usually you can drop a tab of LSD and you will definitely feel the effects by doing this. However with Nbome you have to allow it some time to absorb as stomach acid destroys it. The most common method of doing this is to allow the blotter to rest under your tongue or in between your gum and lip for several minutes. If you drop a blotter and feel nothing then you know that was either just a plain blotter or it was Nbome. LSD is usually handled in a very cautious manner such as it is kept in aluminum foil and tweezers or disposable gloves are used by the dealer to break off hits. This is done because LSD is readily absorbed through the skin. Nbome blotters can be handled very well with just bare skin without risking tripping balls.

Usually Nbome is priced fairly cheap. If you find someone selling LSD cheaper than $10 a hit then I would be cautious as to what it really is. I can go out and buy 900 hits of Nbome for about $350. I can get it a lot cheaper if I lay it on paper myself but this is a difficult process. I do not recommend anyone to lay their own Nbome blotters unless they have a background in chemistry and have access to a microgram scale. A microgram scale will read down to .0000 grams. They are very expensive. Nbome is active at amounts you will have trouble seeing. Usually anywhere from 750-1000 micrograms is the normal dosing on a blotter. This means .75-1 milligram. Do you realize how little substance that is.

A 1milligram Nbome blotter is a very good trip. I would not even recommend this much for a first time user unless you have had prior psychedelic experience.

Nbome related deaths have happened. The most common reason is because people are unaware of how much they are taking. It is possible for you to dip your fingertip in a bag of powder and come out with over 100 milligrams. This would be equal to 100 1 miligram Nbome blotters. That is nowhere near a good idea. That will most definitely result in death. It is important to be cautious and invest in a microgram scale(.0000) if you plan on messing around and laying your own blotters.

LSD and Nbome are quite active at microgram levels. A very nice size hit of LSD I would equate to 200 micrograms. A very nice size hit of Nbome I would equate to 1000 micrograms or 1 milligram. It is important to know how potent these compounds are. They are not to be taken lightly. On the Road you can buy single blotters or full sheets that most likely have been laid correctly and are labeled with the amount of product each dose has. On the Road you can also buy Nbome powder. It is cheaper but leave that shit alone, unless you have the proper equipment to dose it you will most likely end up dead.

Another thing to remember is that even though items are labeled correctly they should not be abused. Nbome is a relatively new chemical and I don't think any research into its side effects have been conducted. It is possible to build up a tolerance. I know a guy who started with one every weekend and within a two month period was ingesting 4 blotters at once.

On the contrary I know a guy who bought 2 from me, three hours later he bought and ingested 2 more. He was up for almost two days straight. His exact words were" Im done with it dude. I watched my life boil before my eyes while I skateboarded to Alaska being chased by wolves." Which I translated into he had an overwhelming experience and he got lost take his dog for a walk on his skateboard in December. He left it alone for a few months but every now and then he would buy a few for him and friends.

That is some crazy shit because according to drug forums that was an extremely large dose and he could have easily died. Chemicals affect different people different ways. This guy has had experience with many other drugs including psychedelics so I attribute this to his survival. So remember when you are messing with chemicals such as Nbome you stay smart about it and don't overdo it and you should be fine.

I remember my first Nbome purchase. I bought a 100 sheet listing for about $120. It arrived fairly quickly. Like 2 days after I ordered it. I realized the guy was only two states away from me so this might have been why. It was in a regular looking envelope. I opened the envelope to reveal it simply was a folded piece of paper containing a small baggie which contained the sheet of bomb. It was weird because I thought blotters had to be kept on aluminum foil to avoid leaking and absorbing into something.

Apparently Nbome is a pretty hardy chemical and can withstand heat to a degree but also requires some moisture to start leaking from the paper which holds it. Wow that's pretty cool right? It'll fuck your ass up if your not careful and take to much so be smart and be safe.

LSD is a lot more forgiving if you accidentally ingest too much. But at the same time you don't want to experience what being Jesus feels like. Too much might turn you into one of those cult leaders or into another Charlie Manson! Seriously just have fun on the weekends with it and don't make it a habit. LSD is fun. Its like nothing else. There are similarities between LSD and Nbome but if you've done both then you would definitely rather have the LSD.

LSD will lead you an a journey that can take you to many different destinations. It can lead you to what your true purpose in life is. However I have found my true purpose in life without it and you can too. It can be a great tool in a class debate. (I don't recommend this though!) It can make your dog look funny. You will be able to taste the separate molecules and minerals that make up the water you are drinking.

It can make you stay up and very awake past your bedtime. You will probably look like shit the next day though so make sure you aren't strung up for a whole day. I hate that shit. I have never liked doing it without having someone to share the experience with. This is because I have tripped without somebody to talk to and I just couldn't help talking to myself in my mind. This could very well be a bad thing.

I have successfully sold thousands of hits of Nbome and only a few hits of LSD. The reason being Nbome is more readily available so it cost me a lot less than LSD. Unlike LSD it is a hardy chemical and can withstand being in a hot car for a few hours without breaking down. I eventually started purchasing whole sheets for around $350 and I resold as follows. Single hits:$8, 100 hits $4 each, Less than 100 hits but more than 50 went for $5 each, all this was early on. Very soon I found myself practically selling a sheet a week to some very happy resellers for $2 each. That's $1800 minus the $350 I paid for it. Do the math and times that by about 4-5 sheets a month. My entire Silk Road drug dealing career lasted only 5 months but in that time period I made more than 6 years salary at my current $8.5 an hour job.

Sells would usually happen like this: I could take about 50 hits and fold it and place it behind a piece of gum. It fit perfectly and while Im walking down the street or sometimes inside of Wal-Mart I would randomly spot a friend and offer them a piece of gum, we would walk and talk and part ways with a handshake. Call me Johnny smooth. For larger purchases I made sure not to get my prints on the sheet and handed it over wrapped up in a paper towel. I placed it in the paper towel in case someone was about to get busted they could simply burn the evidence and hopefully not get charged with the psychedelic. This was and still is a good idea so don't doubt me. Then whoever bought it can place it in a baggy or however they wish to hold it.

Thousands of kids in my county and surrounding county were introduced to Nbome by me. I am happy because I know all those people have had some fun times because of the mysterious little piece of paper. It makes me feel warm and fuzzy just thinking about it.

I tried Nbome twice. The first time was to see how intense it was and believe me I was not expecting a 1mg hit to be that powerful. Like I wanted it to end so bad. I think I went shellshock for a little while. Some crazy shit. Nbome was specifically designed to watch movies on Netflix. All the crazy swirling designs and funny faces made me laugh. You should try it sometime.

LSD on the other hand is rather expensive. I bought 100 hits at about $750 and had a difficult time explaining differences between the two to some people. This blotters cheaper and is a pretty trippy substance but this is the real acid and I'm selling it for twice as much as the other one. This was pretty much a waste for me. I think I would've been able to sell it all if I hadn't been trying to sell the Nbome blotters at the same time. But that wouldn't have brought nearly as much profit as the Nbome though so I'm not to mad about my loss.

My experiences with LSD are going to remain private for now. I will inform you that most of this chapter was written during the last few hours of an LSD trip though. I might write a separate book on that subject because it is unlike anything I have ever experienced and I don't think I should have to share my awesome experiences here for free. It truly is a mind opening substance and should not be used just to "trip".

CHAPTER 7

A GLOSSARY OF TERMS I THINK YOU SHOULD KNOW!

Silk Road Marketplace: The online, hidden, anonymous marketplace where illicit substances can be purchased through an escrow system.

Dread Pirate Roberts: The man responsible for creating the Silk Road Marketplace.

Bitcoins: The digital currency that is allowed as a form of payment on the Silk Road Marketplace. Supposedly anonymous if bought correctly it also is accepted at legal merchants and is gaining popularity.

The Forums: The Silk Road has a dedicated website specifically for forum post regarding practices and news related to the website.

MDMA: a main ingredient in ecstasy tablets, commonly referred to as Molly ,Adam ,rolls, beans, stacks, vitamins

LSD: a powerful psychedelic commonly sold on blotter tabs. Vulnerable to air and light, it is easily absorbed through the skin and precautions should be taken to avoid this. Commonly referred to as acid, cid, Sidney, fluff

Nbome: Relatively new psychedelic which is a derivative of the 2c family. Commonly mislabeled and sold on blotters as LSD. The powder form is available for purchase but is not advised as it is active at sub milligram doses.

Weed: aka cannabis, pot, herb, ganja, green, tree, bud, Buddha, blunt, joint

IRL: term used frequently on The Forums. Stands for In Real Life. As in activities that occur in real life outside of the forum and the Silk Road website.

USPS: The United States Postal Service

DCN: Delivery confirmation number. Green sticker that is usually placed on packages as an alternate means of purchasing tracking numbers.

LEO: Law enforcement officials

Virwex: a scam website that tricks people into purchasing bitcoins way below market value but never actually sending the coins after sending payment.

BMR: stands for Black Market Reloaded. A website similar to Silk Road but it is not nearly as high tech or trustworthy, use at your own risk

The Armory: A website started by Silk Road for the specific purpose of selling firearms and weapons. Shut down due to lack of customers and/or moral purposes.

Controlled Delivery: Is where your delivery is intercepted and LEO attempt to get you to sign for the package to confirm you were the intended recipient. Usually involves LEO posing as your mailman, you sign for it, your door gets kicked in, your house gets searched for evidence related to said package. Make sure your house and computer are clean and deny knowledge of the package and defeating it shouldn't be a problem.

Package Profiling: Basic guidelines Postal Inspectors use to identify packages containing contraband/drugs.

FE: stands for finalize early, never press this button until your order is received. This is the sites way of securing your payment to make sure you get what you paid for and that you don't get scammed. Never FE!

Hidden Wiki: A listing of other websites that can only be accessed through TOR. If you visit any site other than Silk Road you run the risk of getting scammed and losing your money.

Mt.Gox: a very popular bitcoin exchange, the only drawback is that it requires identification verification. It is advised to use the Forums for the most up to date information on obtaining bitcoins anonymously, otherwise this might be your only option.

Tony 76: a vendor on the Road who gained a lot of trust from customers only to pull off a huge scam by making people finalize early on the site for a special sale and then not sending the product.

Anonymous: We are legion!

Love Letter: A letter sent by Customs or the USPS informing you that your package has been found to contain contraband. It is recommended you contact the place from where it was sent and deny knowledge of the package. Your address used for that package is now being watched.

Prison: A place where you will be sent if you are caught with a bunch of drugs, stay smart, stay safe!

Reshippers: Vendors usually have reshippers in other states to throw LEO off the trail of where packages are actually coming from. This is done by placing a package inside a package, sending it to somebody else. That person then removes the hidden package and mails it from a location close to them.

DEA: Drug Enforcement Agency

Domestic: means inside your own country

OS: overseas, means outside of your home country where a package is sent or coming from.

TOR: The onion Router. An ingenious program which allows you to access the internet and no one can see what sites you are visiting. It is possible for someone to see that you are using the TOR program.

Blockchain: All bitcoin transactions are recorded and displayed in almost real time on blockchain.info You can also open up a bitcoin wallet(a place to store your bitcoins)

Stealth: practices a vendor uses to ensure your order reaches you. These methods should not be discussed to anyone. Only you and the vendor should know how an item was packed. If it was made public it would then be possible for LEO to catch on to a vendors shipping methods and intercept his packages.

CHAPTER **8**

CATEGORIES OF THE SILK ROAD ANONYMOUS MARKETPLACE.

This chapter I will go over all the categories that are available on the Road and what you can find in each one.

Apparel: You can find t-shirts and custom bags designed by people for sale in exchange for bitcoins.

ART: Under this category you can find blotter art. Blotter art consist of full size sheets of custom designs. It is possible to request custom blotters. Everything from hentai to Scooby Doo can be put on perforated blotter paper.

Books: Everything from paperback to digital copies of books can be purchased here on a variety of subject matter. I once bought a digital download of the US Marines Basic Combat Training Manual. Now I don't get my lunch money stolen!

Collectibles: You can buy moonshine and collectible artwork from vendors on this page. Moonshine? Yes moonshine is a collectible. It embodies the American Spirit!

Computer Equipment: Visit this page to purchase everything from Bootable Usb sticks which can load the TOR program on the go to thermal printers to encrypted external hard drives the latest Intel Processors.

Custom Orders: This page is usually reserved for custom listings which are setup by your vendor. Say you want to buy something but you don't quite have the cash needed, you talk to the vendor and he agrees to setup a custom listing for a percentage of the product in exchange for what funds you have available.

Digital Goods: This page allows you to purchase everything from hacked Netflix accounts to the latest software from big companies at a fraction of the price. Where else can you buy a version of Adobe Photoshop 6 for under $10?

Drug Paraphenelia: The name says it all. I haven't seen too many big bongs for sale but if you are looking for crack stems, meth pipes, DMT pipes or small hand pipes for weed then look no further.

Drugs: The reason you came to the Road in the first place. Everything from weed to steroids are available for purchase. There are even sub categories for most drugs. Looking for hash or BHO, there's a category for that. Looking for Benzos specifically then there is a category for that. Just try not to get hooked on crack or opium!

Electronics: Everything from night vision goggles, to encrypted laptops to home surveillance systems and signal jammers can be bought here! Don't forget to purchase a GPS tracker to find out why your wife or girlfriend takes so long getting home from work some days!

Erotica: Access hacked accounts from some of the largest and highest quality pornographic websites to gigabytes of porn that can be downloaded to your desktop! Toys are available as well.

Fireworks: Not as many fireworks as Id like to see. The occasional M-80 does pop up though.

Food: Honey caramels, water kefir, and the Original Thailand Red Bull fomula for half the price than Amazon are just a few of the fine foods available for purchase on the darkweb.

Forgeries: You need a pair of Beats Headphones without spending an arm and a leg? How about some designer shades? Other items are available as well.

Hardware: Biometric fingerprint locks, Smith and Wesson handcuff keys, upto 20lb tanks of nitrous oxide are available here.

Home and Garden: Incense, 2 liter bottles of Purell, and sheets of Mylar are down this aisle.

Lab Supplies: Graduated cylinders, silver nitrate, and LSD synthesis guides are just a few of the wonderful lab supplies available. It is recommended that you go here to purchase a Marquis Reagent Test Kit if you plan on buying drugs outside of Silk Road.

Lotteries and Games: Ever bought a ticket for a raffle and the grand prize was 10 hits of LSD? You have now!

Medical: Sterile needles, sutures, injectable Benadryl are just a few of the quality items are available for purchase here.

Money: Having trouble purchasing coins or do you need to cash out your bitcoins without going thru an exchange site? Stop by here and make it happen. Id be cautious of someone requesting cash by mail though.

Packaging: Need vacuum packaging materials or the foil heat sealed packaging that virtually leaves smells undetectable? How about a brand new vacuum sealing machine? Look no further than the packaging category.

Services: Do you need decoy mail sent to see if your roommate has been stealing your ecstasy shipments? How about purchasing a coupon collection which has printable coupons for thousands of in store items.

Tickets: You probably would be better off going to Ticketmaster as there doesn't appear to be a lot of listings in the section.

Weight Loss: Weight loss drinks and supplements are available here. Some of these are only available with a prescription so be careful with what you decide to use.

Writing: Felt like getting high all semester and now you need an intelligent classmate to help you write something for your senior graduation project? For a fee and sometime to research you can have someone with a college degree do it for you. Poems are available for purchase as well.

CHAPTER **9**

MY CLOSING ARGUMENTS FOR THE SILK ROAD MARKETPLACE.

Let me start off by saying that my experience using this unique website has definitely had a huge impact on my life. I have had my mind opened by ideas of revolutionaries and LSD. It is a great place even if it is mostly made up of drug dealers and hackers. Just the idea of this website in general is something that you should respect.

I must say that I do not condone any illegal activities and this book was written for entertainment purposes only. It is possible for you to get into a lot of trouble with some of the items that are for sale. It is extremely easy to catch 20 years just by picking up a package of drugs out of your mailbox. Be smart and stay safe. Think about it before you act. Is it really worth risking your freedom? Is it really worth not risking your freedom and letting laws tell you what to do?

There are many sides to this argument. Personally I love the idea of this website. I don't like the fact that I was caught with more than a few grams of MDMA and had to turn into a confidential informant to save myself from a hefty prison sentence. That's right, I bitched out. I had a great excuse. First of all I didn't get caught with drugs in my mailbox. An argument escalated into a police visit and subsequent search of my residence. When pulled aside by an officer and asked if I would like to "work" I immediately said yes.

How could I possibly snitch out a stranger you ask? I didn't. I simply wore a wire a few times and got some local heroin and crack dealers busted. The mysterious ecstasy connect magically appeared again when one of the dealers was found to be in possession of MDMA caps that appeared similar to the ones I was busted with. He bought them from a friend of mine I had introduced to on the side and out of sight of my police handler.

I feel bad but this is a dog eat dog world and it had to be done. I consider myself lucky to have been able to mastermind my way out of this. I think I am in the clear because I do not think my local dealers realized the man I had introduced them to was my police handler and that I had been flipped by law enforcement. I did serve some time on the other charges in the form of probation.

Like I said before I consider myself lucky and if you plan on using the Road to conduct business be wise in your decisions IRL. You could end up in a position like me but you either won't have anybody else to throw under the bus or you simply choose not to.

I for one am done with the Road. Not because of this bust but because I had already trained my resellers on its use and was simply selling off some leftover product. I got plenty money saved up but if I could go back and change time I would have never used the Road to purchase drugs. There is too much risk involved for me and this tool is so easy to use a kid could do it.

I hope my book has made you aware of some of the risk and rewards available for those who tempt fate in our technological world. Think before you act. Be smart and stay safe.

Johnny Blazed
March 27, 2013

PS: Lookout for my new book where I actually go into detail about my bust and write about it on more than 155 pages of text. I am a stoner and I dint want to take a long time to write this book. Did you know that some people take years to write a book? Yeah right.